The Story of Ellis Island

Not like the brazen giant of Greek fame,
With conquering limbs astride from land to land;
Here at our sea-washed, sunset gates shall stand
A mighty woman with a torch, whose flame
Is the imprisoned lightning, and her name
Mother of Exiles. From her beacon-hand
Glows world-wide welcome; her mild eyes command
The air-bridged harbor that twin cities frame.
"Keep ancient lands, your storied pomp!" cries she
With silent lips. "Give me your tired, your poor,
Your huddled masses yearning to breathe free,
The wretched refuse of your teeming shore.
Send these, the homeless, tempest-tost to me,
I lift my lamp beside the golden door!"

"The New Colossus,"
written by Emma Lazarus in 1883.

OTHER BOOKS BY WILLARD A. HEAPS

Riots, U.S.A. 1765-1965
The Wall of Shame
The Bravest Teenage Yanks

THE STORY OF

Ellis Island

Willard A. Heaps

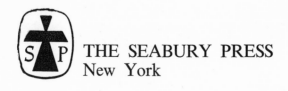

THE SEABURY PRESS
New York

ACKNOWLEDGMENT

Grateful acknowledgment is made to the publishers and author for permission to use copyrighted material from:

A Nation of Immigrants by John F. Kennedy. Harper & Row, N.Y. Copyright © 1964 by the Anti-Defamation League of B'nai B'rith.

Contents

1

The Gateway

⚑ The formal opening of the Ellis Island Immigrant Station, less than half a mile from the Statue of Liberty in New York Harbor, took place on Friday, January 1, 1892. Three large steamships had been waiting at their piers to unload their steerage passengers. The transfer boat *John E. Moore,* gaily decorated for the occasion, approached the Island's landing, carrying 148 steerage passengers from the S.S. *Nevada* amid "the clang of bells and the din of shrieking whistles."

A 15-year-old, rosy-cheeked Irish girl, Annie Moore, from County Cork, was nearest to the gangplank when it was lowered. She was the first to be questioned in the second-floor registry room. The waiting officials presented her with a $10 gold piece and, according to the *Times,* "she had never seen a United States coin and this was the largest sum of money she had ever possessed."

Annie was bringing her two younger brothers to join their parents, who had immigrated to New York four years before.

Seven hundred passengers from the *City of Paris* and the *Victoria* were also cleared that day.

The Island was in operation.

The clearance process at Ellis Island was designed to determine whether or not, under the terms of the immigration laws, an alien should be allowed to enter the United States. Those who came knocking at America's door generally considered it as the final step in a long series, going back to the time when they first made their decision to journey into the unknown future, which for most would terminate in their becoming citizens.

Ellis Island was many things to many people. Several different phrases have been used to describe it:

—a "gateway" to what most of those passing through considered the promised land, the "threshold to a new life."

—"the Golden Door," the term first used in *The New Colossus,* the famous poem by Emma Lazarus.

—a "turnstile," because of its control and counting function.

—a "sorting depot" or a "sieve," because of its determination of who would be accepted and who rejected.

From the earliest colonial days regulation and inspection of immigrants had been the responsibility of the individual state where the point of entry was located. The federal government passed no laws on immigration until 1819, and that law covered only rules and standards regarding steerage conditions on sailing vessels. Also, it made the first provision that statistics and records be kept regarding immigration. Amendments to the law were passed in 1847 and 1848; they too were limited to sailing vessels.

From 1820 until 1882 immigration regulations were enacted by various states, but none of the provisions were uniform. Time and again the state laws were declared unconstitutional by the Supreme Court on the ground that they violated the right of Congress to regulate foreign commerce, as stated in the Constitution.

In 1876, a Supreme Court decision for the first time recommended that Congress should exercise full authority over immigration, mainly so that standard laws would be in force. "We are of the opinion," said the justices, "that this whole subject of immigration has been confided to Congress by the Constitution; that Congress can more appropriately and with more acceptance exercise it than any other body known to our law, state or national; that, by providing a system of laws in these matters applicable to all ports and to all vessels, a serious question which has long been a matter of contest and complaint may be effectively and satisfactorily settled." Though bills were introduced in both houses of Congress for the national regulation of immigration, no legislation was enacted until 1882.

This first federal immigration law established federal supervision and provided for a head tax* of fifty cents to be levied on all aliens landing at United States ports. The Secretary of the Treasury was charged with carrying out the act; for that purpose he was given authority to enter into contracts with the appropriate state officers, who would continue to take charge of local immigration.

Congressional dissatisfaction with the manner in which the states carried out their contracted obligations re-

* The head tax was originally levied by individual states to aid in meeting the expenses of immigrant reception. When the government assumed the full responsibility for the administration of immigration in 1891, the sum was increased to $1. Subsequent laws raised the sum to $2, $4, and finally, in 1918, $8. The head tax was not abolished until 1952, when it was replaced by a $25 charge for a visa.

sulted in 1890 in an official inquiry into all phases of the immigration problem. The result was a law in 1891 which authorized the appointment of a Superintendent of Immigration under the Treasury Department.* This law, which also spelled out in detail the inspection procedures, was based on the "exclusive power of the federal government to regulate commerce." The odd "commerce" phrase, of course, referred not to the alien passengers but to the steamship companies which had steadfastly fought any and all suggestions of federal control and supervision.

New York City had always been the port of entry for by far the largest number of immigrants. In 1855 Castle Garden, an ancient fort on the lower tip of Manhattan Island at the Battery which had been used for many years as a theatre, was designated as an immigration station under state supervision, with a hospital on Ward's Island opposite 103d Street in the East River. When the federal law was passed in 1882, the Castle Garden station continued to operate under contract to the United States government.

By 1890 the facilities of Castle Garden had long since proved inadequate for the ever-increasing number of arrivals. Concurrently with the Congressional inquiry, government officials took over the operation of the station, meanwhile conducting a survey of the New York Harbor area

* The Bureau of Immigration was a branch of the Treasury Department until 1903, when it was transferred to the Department of Commerce and Labor, with the title Superintendent changed to Commissioner-General. When naturalization functions were assigned to the Bureau in 1906, it became the Bureau of Immigration and Naturalization. The Bureau became a division of the newly created Department of Labor in 1913, and was consolidated into the Immigration and Naturalization Service in 1933. In 1940 the latter was transferred to the Department of Justice.

in order to locate a site on which to establish an entirely new United States Immigrant Station.

Ellis Island was their choice. Early in the search, the idea of a site in Manhattan was rejected because of the difficulties encountered at Castle Garden. Immigrants landing there had been ruthlessly exploited when they left the station, and the transport of the newcomers to the various railroad terminals in both Manhattan and New Jersey was difficult. On an island the immigrants could be both protected and guided.

Located a short distance from the New Jersey shore in upper New York Bay, Ellis Island, between three and four acres in size, was known to the Indians as Gull Island. Because of the delicious oysters found off its shores when Manhattan Island was under the Dutch, it was called Oyster Island and for almost 150 years it continued to be a favorite resort for picnics, oyster roasts, clam bakes and fishing parties. By means never officially determined, it finally passed into the hands of one Samuel Ellis, presumably a New Jersey farmer of that name. When he died in 1794, the island was taken over by New York state, probably for nonpayment of taxes, and called Bucking Island.

The site was considered so excellent for the defense of the harbor that it was purchased by the federal government. After first being used as a powder magazine and arsenal, it was subsequently fortified. In 1807 Fort Gibson, a full-scale stronghold, was erected; it was defended by 15 guns and manned by a garrison of 80 men. The fort was dismantled in 1861, and the name of Ellis Island again adopted.

The Island was used as a naval munitions magazine

until in 1890 it was chosen by the House Committee on Immigration as the site of the new Immigrant Station for the Port of New York.

When the Island was finally selected, an appropriation of $150,000 was authorized for improvements and buildings. While construction was taking place in 1890 and 1891, the Barge Office on the Battery near the closed Castle Garden was used for immigrant reception. The Barge Office had been the landing place for immigrants arriving from the steamship piers and en route to Castle Garden nearby, and was for many years the terminal for the Ellis Island ferryboats.

The first buildings for the new Immigrant Station were constructed of Georgia pine, with slate roofs. The largest was the three-story reception building, through which every alien passed. Four-story peaked towers marked the corners of this building, characterized at the time as a "ramshackle pavilion."

Smaller buildings included a dormitory for detainees, a small hospital, a restaurant, a baggage station and a power house. One side of the Island, the southern, had been reinforced by a sea wall, and it formed the landing stage for the transfer boats (or barges, as they were called) which were to bring the steerage passengers from the docked liners, and for the ferry which transported those bound for New York to the Barge Office at the Battery.

The first personnel of the Island were taken over from the state's Castle Garden operation. When all positions were classed under the federal civil service around the turn of the century, most of the higher positions were filled by examination, though the office of Commissioner was for many years a political appointment.

The number of employees varied according to the immigrant ebb and flow, the average being about five hundred. In peak periods as many as 850 were at work (most "commuted" from Manhattan), and even then the Island was understaffed. At other times, such as during the two wars, only 100 were retained. The personnel included immigration officers, interpreters, dozens of clerks, guards, matrons, gatekeepers, watchmen, cooks, etc., as well as maintenance employees, such as engineers, firemen, painters, charwomen and gardeners. The huge medical staff numbered scores of physicians, inspectors, nurses and orderlies. Indeed, Ellis Island was almost a self-contained and independent city.

The life of the first station was short, for all of the flimsy frame buildings on the Island were burned to the ground in a disastrous fire on June 15, 1897. Congress immediately appropriated $600,000 to replace the structures with fireproof buildings; during the next two and a half years the processing of immigrants was again conducted at the Barge Office.

The new fireproof buildings, brick and ironwork structures with limestone trimmings, were occupied in December, 1900. The main building, 338 feet long and 168 feet wide, was somewhat Oriental in appearance; it was notable for its four cupola-type towers and the large, light and airy second floor Registry Room. On the floor above (back from the balconies overlooking this room) were dormitories. The other floors housed administrative offices, record rooms, special inquiry board hearing rooms and railroad ticket offices. The entire first floor was used as a receiving room for the baggage of arriving aliens.

North of this building was a large baggage room and dormitory building for those who were detained for long periods.

Throughout the years the original Island of 3½ acres was enlarged by fill into three man-made islands, with boat slips between. They were connected on the western sides by filled land. The original Island was increased to ten acres at the time of the rebuilding. The three-acre Island Number 2, constructed from 1900 to 1902, included a huge many-winged hospital, a new restaurant and a bathhouse. This hospital, administered by the United States Public Health Service (originally called the Marine Health Service), was considered one of the best in the country and was always given a grade A rating by the American Medical Association.

In 1913 a five-acre third island was added to the south, with additional hospital structures where patients with various contagious diseases were isolated. At the time it was abandoned in 1954, the Island covered 27½ acres and included 35 buildings, some of which had not been used for two or more decades.

The Ellis Island Immigrant Station was almost blown out of existence on July 30, 1916, at the time of the Black Tom explosions on the New Jersey shore only a few hundred yards away. Black Tom Island was a railroad yard and barge loading area. Dynamite and munitions, loaded on railroad cars and on 14 barges awaiting transfer to freighters which would take them to Russia, were exploded by saboteurs who were never apprehended. Two separate shocks were of such force that they were felt in Philadelphia, 90 miles away; and for several hours after, smaller explosions erupted as boxes of bullets, shrapnel, bombs and shells were ignited.

Nearly five hundred immigrants and 125 employees were asleep on Ellis Island when the blasts, resembling the sound of big guns, were set off at about two o'clock in the morning. The flaming sky, the deafening explosions and detonations of shells panicked the aliens, many of whom thought the war, which they had escaped, had followed them. Almost all windows had been broken immediately, the doors had been jammed inward and parts of the roofs had collapsed.

The incoming tide moved the burning barges with their exploding cargoes toward the Island. By some miracle the staff were able to lead the lightly clad aliens, both the healthy and the sick, to the eastern corner of the Island. There, in wild disorder, they were loaded onto the ferries and taken to the Manhattan Barge Office, while five-inch shells flared over the Island like skyrockets.

Fortunately the barges were towed away from the Island, and throughout the morning the New York Fire Department was able to put out the many scattered fires which resulted from the fall of flaming debris. Even so, the damage on Ellis Island amounted to $400,000.

During the First World War, when immigration practically ceased, the Island served as an internment center for 1,500 German sailors and 2,200 suspected aliens and spies. Later the huge hospital was turned over to the War and Navy Departments for the care of wounded soldiers and sailors. At one time almost seven hundred patients taxed the hospital's capacity. After the armistice, the Immigrant Station reverted to its original function.

The first "quota" law restricting immigration was enacted in 1921. Other even more restrictive laws (see Chapter 11) resulted in the flood of arrivals at Ellis Island being reduced to a comparative trickle. Not only were fewer immigrants received but beginning in 1925 their examination for clearance, under the 1924 law, was made by the United States Consuls in their homelands, who issued them certificates of entry.

Proposals to close Ellis Island were made as early as 1925, but immigrant processing did not cease entirely until 1932, when only 21,500 aliens in all classes arrived in New York. The previously obtained certificates of the immigrants were thereafter examined by officers on the steamship piers; and the Island became a place of detention for immigrants who arrived ill or whose papers were not in order, or those who were to be deported.

2

Emigration from Europe

🖐 Annie Moore was the first of over 16 million immigrants to pass through Ellis Island during its forty years (1892-1932) as an immigrant reception station. In recognition of its importance in the story of our country, the Island was designated as a part of the Statue of Liberty National Monument by a proclamation which President Lyndon B. Johnson signed in a White House ceremony on May 11, 1965.

Ellis Island is a part of the experience of millions of today's Americans, whose passage through it was the first step toward attaining citizenship. Ellis Island is also a focal point in the family histories of additional millions whose relatives or ancestors entered the United States as immigrants through the Port of New York.

In terms of volume alone, Table 1 at the end of this chapter indicates for a selected number of years (when the official reporting was uniform) the role played by Ellis Island in both the national and local (New York) phases of immigration.

The 16 million Ellis Island immigrants came mostly from Europe, and they formed about 70 per cent of the 23 million who entered the country during the four decades of

its operation. Even more startling is the fact that they constituted 38 per cent of the grand total of the nearly 42
million aliens who have arrived in the United States since
the federal statistical records were first compiled in 1820.
An average of between 85 and 90 per cent of all immigrants arriving in New York between 1892 and 1932
were steerage passengers. Under the law they were all
without exception required to pass through the Island,
where they were screened before being admitted to the
United States. Before restrictive immigration laws were
passed after the First World War, as many as a million
immigrants arriving in steerage were processed annually,
as in 1907. In four years—1905, 1906, 1910 and 1914—
the annual number was over three quarters of a million. On
days when several large ships, each carrying over a thousand passengers in steerage, docked concurrently, the number passing through within a single day was five thousand
or more, an average of two per minute.

Only a few immigrant passengers (from ten to fifteen
per cent) from the two cabin classes were detained by health
and immigration inspectors at quarantine and sent to Ellis
Island for further checks.

The story of the Island, therefore, is the story of the
steerage immigrants, those who were characterized in Emma
Lazarus' poem "The New Colossus," which is engraved on
a tablet inside the pedestal of the Statue of Liberty, as
"tired . . . poor . . . huddled masses yearning to breathe
free."

Though Ellis Island was by far the largest and most
important, more than 70 other federal immigrant stations
were located along the boundaries and shores of the United

States. Immigrants from Latin America landed at New Or-
leans, Savannah and other Gulf and South Atlantic ports;
Chinese and other Orientals landed at San Francisco, Seattle
and other Pacific Coast ports; and Mexicans crossed the
border into Texas, New Mexico, Arizona, or California.

The majority of New York arrivals were naturally from
the Old World, but many other European immigrants,
particularly from the Northern countries, landed in Canada
and crossed the border to the United States. Other Atlantic
ports such as Boston, Philadelphia and Baltimore received
many thousands from Europe, but the number was insig-
nificant in comparison with the Port of New York.

An accepted definition of "immigration" from the social
science point of view was expressed by the distinguished
sociologist Henry Pratt Fairchild in his 1913 book *Immigration: A World Movement and Its American Significance:* "a movement of people, individually or in families,
acting on their own personal initiative and responsibility,
without official support or compulsion, passing from one
country (usually old and thickly settled) to another (usually
new and sparsely settled) with the intention of residing there
permanently."

Immigration has flowed toward America in a series of
continuous waves. The size and diversity of our foreign-born
population has caused us to be termed "a nation of immigrants."

From the early days of the colonies America has needed,
even wooed, newcomers who have built the country from a
wilderness to one of the most powerful and prosperous
nations of the world.

The 1953 report of the Commission on Immigration and

Naturalization appointed by President Harry Truman to establish policy on future immigration stated the debt of the United States to its immigrant population in these words: "Our growth as a nation has been achieved, in large measure, through the genius and industry of immigrants of every race and from every quarter of the world. The story of their pursuit of happiness is the saga of America. Their brains and their brawn helped to settle our land, to advance our agriculture, to build our industries, to develop our commerce, to produce new inventions and, in general, to make us the leading nation that we now are. . . . Historically speaking, immigration has supplied much of the brain and sinew, the human resources that have created our nation."

Emphasizing chronology, historians have characterized the human flow to the United States from Europe as "colonists" (those who reached America before 1776), the "old" immigration, and the "new" immigration.

The "old" immigration, those who arrived between 1820 (when federal statistics of origin were first recorded) and 1880, was almost entirely made up of northwest Europeans. More specifically, the people of the "old" immigration came from England, Ireland, Scotland, Wales, Belgium, Denmark, France, Germany, the Netherlands, Norway, Sweden and Switzerland.

The "new" immigration, which began in the 1880s, came to this country from southern and southeastern European countries, including Austria-Hungary, Bulgaria, Greece, Italy, Montenegro, Poland, Rumania, Russia, Serbia and Turkey.

The shift from the "old" to the "new" before the enactment of restrictive legislation is succinctly shown in Table 2 at the end of this chapter.

The reasons for which the various national groups of Europe immigrated to the United States and the peak years of their arrival, which indicate the crests of the waves of both the "old" and "new" immigration, are concisely discussed in John F. Kennedy's *A Nation of Immigrants.* Both as Senator and President, John Kennedy, whose paternal great-grandfather emigrated from Ireland to Boston in 1848, was interested in the correction of inequities in our immigration laws. His 1963 study of the problem while preparing to introduce reforms, which were finally enacted in 1965, was published posthumously in 1964.

President Kennedy characterized the motivations of each nationality and the peak years of their arrival.

"Frenchmen cried, 'Let us rule ourselves; our kings are not divine!' To date, estimated immigration from France: 698,188. Peak year, 1851.

"The bold, imaginative Irish left their land during the years of famine for the land of opportunity. Estimated immigration from Ireland to date: 4,693,009. Peak decade: 1851-1860.

"From Germany came the liberals and those who fled persecution [for their political beliefs]. Estimated immigration from Germany to date: 6,798,313. Peak decade: 1881-1890.

"To the Midwest the Scandinavians [coming for economic reasons] brought their knowledge of agriculture. Estimated total: 2,453,494. Peak year: 1882. From Denmark, 354,331; from Norway, 843,867; from Sweden, 1,255,296.

"From Great Britain came Pilgrims, who sought freedom; Quakers, who loved their brothers but who were not allowed to love them in peace; sturdy Scots and Welsh [They sought a new life with those who spoke the same language]. To date, estimated immigration from Great Britain: 4,642,096. Peak year: 1888.

"Fleeing Czarist and Communist suppression, came an estimated 3,344,998 from Russia, some forty per cent of them Jews fleeing persecution. Peak decade: 1901-1910.

"The Greeks found soil where vineyards might flourish. To date, estimated immigration from Greece: 499,465. Peak year: 1907.

"From Austria-Hungary, whose empire was cut into bits and pieces, whole villages banded together to find a new life. To date, estimated immigration from Austria and Hungary: 4,280,863. Peak year: 1907.

"Italians settled in the cities of the East and the valleys of the West. To date, estimated immigration from Italy: 5,017,625. Peak year: 1907."

Why did these millions emigrate from Europe? Though the decision to come to America was highly individual, the motives were fundamentally the same for all newcomers—religious persecution, political oppression, or economic hardship. As Mr. Kennedy states in his book, "They were responding, in their own way, to the pledge of the Declaration of Independence: the promise of 'life, liberty and the pursuit of happiness.' "

Maldwyn Jones, whose study *American Immigration* is a standard work, writes that "the motives for immigration have been very similar from first to last; they have been always a mixture of yearnings—for riches, for land, for change, for tranquillity, for freedom, and for something not definable in words. . . . The story of American Immigration is one of millions of enterprising, courageous folk, most of them humble, nearly all of them unknown by name to history. Coming from a great variety of backgrounds, they nonetheless resembled one another in their willingness to look beyond the horizon and in their readiness to pull up stakes in order to seek a new life."

Quite naturally, the major hope of all male immigrants was to find better work; and to America they brought their skills, their trades and their willingness to work. The vast expansion of American industry in the late nineteenth and early twentieth centuries created an unprecedented demand for cheap and unskilled labor. The male "new" immigrants, sturdy and accustomed to hard work, were not only needed but welcomed. The foreign-born formed the mass of wage earners in mining and manufacturing where, even with the mass influx, the supply seldom matched the ever-growing demand.

The 16 million who passed through Ellis Island consisted overwhelmingly of "new" immigrants, and they formed the all-time peak of all the various immigration waves, as shown in Table 2 at the end of this chapter.

Throughout its operation, Ellis Island continued to receive thousands of the "old" immigrants, though in numbers greatly reduced from the pre-1890 peaks. However, because of the preponderance of eastern and southern European immigrants, the story of Ellis Island, in addition to being that of steerage passengers, is the story of the "new" immigration.

The newcomers who arrived in such astronomical numbers were overwhelmingly young, with the family-producing years in their futures. Official statistics (compiled from 1906 through 1910) indicate that only five per cent of the European steerage immigrants were 45 or over. Twelve per cent were under 14; these included the babes in arms and the young children who grew up in their new country, in turn becoming parents themselves.

The largest age group, 14 to 45 years, accounted for over 82 per cent. Many of these, in the younger age brackets, would either marry and have families or, if already married, would increase the number of their children.

The majority of the millions who passed through the Island, most of them to become citizens, would be absorbed into the fabric of American life. Almost all would make a contribution, however anonymous and unnoticed, to the development of their new country. Most would remain relatively unknown in their adopted land; some would attain local distinction and prominence.

Some were destined for national, even worldwide, fame, including Irving Berlin from Russia; football immortal Knute Rockne from Norway; Supreme Court Justice Felix Frankfurter from Austria; labor leader Philip Murray from Scotland; Father Edward Flanagan, founder of the famous Boys Town, from Ireland; Spyros Skouras, motion picture executive, and Elia Kazan, stage and film director, from Greece. Most of these immigrants were too young when they arrived to remember much of their Ellis Island experiences. Mr. Berlin and Mr. Kazan, for example, were both four at the time.

For personal accounts, therefore, the author interviewed several dozen people in their sixties, seventies and eighties in the New York City area, where Ellis Island "alumni" may be found in abundance. These senior citizens uniformly agreed that their arrival in the United States and their experience at the Island, whether of a few hours or a few days' duration, was a high point in their lives. Their memories of the distant experience of coming to America, as recorded on tape, were almost uncanny in detail.

A writer for the National Park Service, in urging in 1964 that Ellis Island be designated as a national monument, expressed its significance by drawing a parallel. "To almost everyone who passed through it, and their descendants as well," the writer stated, "Ellis Island has been as important in fact as Plymouth Rock has now become in fancy for the descendants of those who came in the first colonization wave."

The way was seldom easy; and the stories of emigration from the mother country to the new land of promise have become family sagas, told and retold.

An elderly Russian who had changed his multisyllabic, unpronounceable name to Boris Treschoff when he became a naturalized American citizen, told of his father's reasons for coming to the United States. Boris was only eight at the time, 1897, but remembers in detail what his father explained to him many times during his youth and young manhood.

"My father used to say that we were serfs bound to a heartless master who cared nothing about us and barely knew we existed. We worked hard and received nothing except the bare necessities. Yes, we were poor and humble. Our only happiness was the family, for like all Jews we were close together. We had been peasants living on the same plot of land for generations. My ancestors were born, lived, worked and died there. They did not dare to think about going to any other place. Where would they go without finding life the same? No, there was no hope anywhere."

Boris Treschoff, now a retired lawyer, continued. "Americans cannot understand what it was like to be a European peasant. . . . Just the other day I was thinking that we were in a way like the Negroes in the South as they were before these new laws gave them hope.

"My father told us that he knew that he could never change his low station [in the Old World] and that he was discontented. Some of our fellow villagers had gone to America a few years before. Their letters, passed from hand to hand, made him think that here was his chance, and the more he thought about it the more determined he was that he would follow them.

"He would argue with Mama and try to tell her that he was right, but she would say that he should go ahead while she would stay with her family. . . . She finally agreed to go with him. They sold everything they had and the estate manager gave us pieces of paper which were the only permission needed to leave Russia and which said we were not running away.

"Now you see what coming here meant to us. Father wanted us to be individuals and was willing to gamble on the future. There was no peasant class as such in America—at least it was not like Russia—and anyone with ambition at least had the chance to better himself. This is exactly what my father, may he ever be blessed, did. It was not easy, not at all, and it took years, but he was able to send me to school, and he used to say that he *knew* he was not a peasant any longer when he was able to send me to college and then law school and give my brothers their businesses.

"This is what America had promised us, and it came true."

TABLE 1. IMMIGRATION THROUGH ALL UNITED STATES POINTS OF ENTRY, THE PORT OF NEW YORK AND ELLIS ISLAND IN SELECTED YEARS

Year	Total U.S.	Port of New York—Total Arrivals	% of U.S. Total	Through Ellis Island Total	% of New York Arrivals
1903	857,046	689,356	80%	631,885	89%
1904	812,870	606,019	74.5%	526,000	86%
1905	1,026,499	821,169	80%	809,847	89%
1907	1,285,349	1,123,842	87%	1,004,756	89%
1911	878,587	749,642	85%	637,003	85%
1912	838,172	725,040	86%	605,161	83%
1913	1,197,892	892,653	74%	767,681	86%
1914	1,218,480	878,052	72%	834,274	95%

NOTE: The difference between the Port of New York and Ellis Island totals represents the number of cabin class passengers who were cleared on the ships.

TABLE 2. ORIGIN OF EUROPEAN IMMIGRATION

Showing Shift from "Old" to "New": % of Total
United States Arrivals

Periods	Northern & Western Europe ("Old")	Southern & Eastern Europe ("New")	All Europe
1821-1880	82	2.5	85
1881-1890	72	18.3	90.3
1891-1900	44.6	51.9	96.5
1901-1910	21.7	70.8	92.5
1911-1920	17.4	58.9	76.3

3

Leaving the Old World

🗡 The prospective emigrant's decision to leave his village and homeland was a critical and momentous one, for it would mean both breaking with the past and beginning a future at best promising with boundless opportunities, at worst uncertain in its unknown problems and challenges.

Advice was freely given by every member of the family. Discussions could become so emotional that the intended emigrant was torn between family duty and obligations and his own plans for the future.

The experience of Stanislaw Mozrowski, who left his home village of Bazlik in pre-World War I Montenegro, was, to quote him, "terrible even to talk about these many years later."

"We Jewish people, as you must know," he began, "are very family-minded. We respect our parents before everything else, and the wisdom and experience of our old people are always worth our attention.

"I was only eighteen then and the oldest son—that was the trouble—and for three or four years I had saved secretly to come to America. My mother was my supporter and from time to time she was able to give me a few halers and an occasional koruna—these were the smallest values [denominations] in our money. But my father would not even let me talk to him about my hopes. My place, he said emphatically, was at home.

"Once in a while my mother would feel that he was in a good mood—wives can sense these things—and she would look at me, put her finger over her mouth as if to say 'don't say anything, let me do the talking,' and start by remarking about something I had done well, and of course he would agree. Then she would begin to talk about my future. He would immediately stiffen, but sometimes she would continue until he would pound on the table and yell 'Silence! No more, do you hear?'

"But we could talk secretly with everyone else, seeking advice and opinions. There was always a story about someone who was already in America enjoying a good life; we in Europe never heard about the troubles there, for everything was rosy. The wise elders and even the rabbi would tell me to leave by all means. I would ask for arguments I could use with my father, for, you see, I loved and respected him and would not for a moment think of leaving him without his blessing.

"Gradually my father's friends began speaking out for me and my father listened politely. Though I had not said so, they told him that I might just run away since I was so determined. They began to wear him down.

"But the family and all the relatives of both my parents had to have their say, and they were hard to convince. The womenfolk supported me, but in our class their opinions were not asked so their influence was nothing. All the men relatives discussed me and my plans endlessly and very soon the family opinion seemed to be turning in my favor. But there still were those who thought I was too young, that I should stay with my parents, that I should be satisfied with a life like theirs, that I should give up my crazy plan or at least postpone it.

"When the decision was made, it came with a bang. It was after the celebration of the Jewish high holy days, when we were observing Succoth, the harvest festival, and we had enjoyed a wonderful meal together. Dearest Momma plunged in and said there had been a lot of talk for weeks and weeks and that I should have their blessing for my journey. It was perfect timing because everyone was happy and sentimental. In no time at all it was decided that I would not only go, but that every branch of the family would make a contribution for my fare to the port, my steerage ticket, and enough money to start out with."

This practice of one member of a family going to America first, then saving to bring others over, had been common among "old"-type immigrants of pre-Ellis Island days. From 1900 to 1910, 94 per cent of the arriving immigrants at Ellis Island stated they were going to join either friends or relatives.

A writer in the 1880s, speaking of New York City, stated, "There is hardly an Irish colleen below stairs who is not regularly putting aside a weekly sum to bring over a sister, with a post waiting in the home of one of the mistress' friends."

Many a father came alone to test the opportunities before sending for his wife and family. The family of George Kazan, including four-year-old Elia, followed him to New

York City after he had proved his success as a rug importer.

In another common pattern an elder son emigrated first, then sent for the next in age, and so on until the entire family was in America. The Skouras brothers came from Greece in this way. Charles, the next to the oldest of four, arrived in 1907, and after three years as a bus boy and bartender in St. Louis, sent passage money to Spyros, who came in 1910 and found a job as bus boy awaiting him. Two years later the two boys sent for their youngest brother, George.

Many of the letters from the United States contained remittances; often these took the form of prepaid tickets, complete from the emigrant's home to the city in America where the sender was waiting.

In 1890 testimony by steamship passenger agents before a Congressional committee revealed that between one-quarter and one-half of all immigrants were arriving on prepaid tickets. In 1901 the United States Industrial Commission found that between 40 and 65 per cent of all immigrants at that time came either on prepaid tickets or on money sent to them by relatives in the United States.

During the peak years of the "new" immigration, from 1903 to 1907 and from 1910 to 1915, the transportation of steerage immigrants was a vast and lucrative business for the steamship companies, even though the average charge was about $30 during the first 15 years of the century. Steerage required no special accommodations and services, and only minimum facilities.

Since the larger ships could accommodate from 1,500

to 2,000 passengers in steerage, a company might receive from $45,000 to $60,000 from such passengers for a single one-way western voyage.

Companies were able to meet the basic costs of the voyage from the much higher revenues of the two cabin classes, leaving the income from steerage as clear profit. The cost of steerage food and crew services was kept minimal: the largest liners could feed one immigrant for sixty cents per day.

In the first 22 years of Ellis Island the $30 average fare was common on both the Mediterranean (15 days) and the North Atlantic (eight to ten days) runs. In times of price wars between steamship lines a special rate of $16 or $15 "per head" was offered as an inducement. By 1915, the steerage fare from Italy was raised to $65. The fares of the North Atlantic Conference, a monopoly of four shipping companies, were slightly raised at that time to $32 for slower ships and $35 on faster ships.

Securing steerage tickets was easy; all tickets were sold without specific space reservations. Passage on a particular ship was obtained only at the port of embarkation. The principal lines operated hundreds of agencies in the United States where passage for relatives and friends could be purchased.

In eastern European countries—Austria-Hungary, Poland, Greece and Russia—thousands of agents traveled from village to village, peddling open tickets in an almost modern "hard sell" manner. By painting an encouraging and highly optimistic picture of employment opportunities in America, they promoted both immigration and ticket sales. Many agents were nattily dressed returned immigrants whose embroidered stories were difficult, if not impossible, to resist.

Once the decision was made and either before or after the ticket was bought, a passport had to be obtained. This the prospective emigrant secured from local and state officials.

He then obtained a United States visa from the nearest American consular office. Peasants in rural areas could get visas from the local consul at the port before sailing. However, certain necessary papers and information had to be prepared before leaving home.

The procedure in Italy was more or less typical, except that tickets were sold only to Italian emigrants who had already obtained passports.

Giuseppe Boldini, who left in 1908, described this process. "A monarchy had representatives of the king in every village," he said. "There always seemed to be a few officials—these were almost always political appointments —who were kept busy making records of everything, absolutely everything. They had birth certificates. They knew our political activities and party membership, our military service record (it was required), any trouble we had been in and what punishment we had received, everything about us. Of course we knew all these men personally and answered any other questions which were needed.

"These papers we took to the *syndic* [mayor], who sent the application to the authorities of the province. It was sent with a *nulla osta,* or 'no objection.' These province men sent the application to the capital, and when the passport arrived, we could apply for the American visa."

Other, less particular countries required only an exit

permit, and the emigrant was responsible for obtaining his passport. Many were the sad tales of peasants who were required to wait at the port of embarkation for days, sometimes weeks, until their passports were issued. Many of the immigrant aid societies established European offices to make sure that every requirement was met before the individual started on his journey.

Even reaching a railroad, much less a port, was often a long and difficult journey for the travelers, most of whom lived in remote rural sections. On foot, on donkey back, in rude wagons and carriages, they traveled until the nearest railway station was reached. The prepaid tickets avoided much confusion and money helped supply comforts.

Almost always there would be someone in a large group who had been over the road before and who would give the others confidence and advice. A substantial number had never before taken a trip by train and many had never left their home villages.

Emigrants from Europe followed two paths to America. Those from southeastern countries such as southern Austria-Hungary, Bulgaria, Greece, Montenegro, Rumania, Serbia and Turkey sailed from Constantinople (now Istanbul), Piraeus in Greece, and Trieste or Fiume on the Adriatic Sea. The Italians sailed from Palermo or Taormina in Sicily, Naples in mid-Italy and Genoa in the north. The journey of those leaving by this Mediterranean route was relatively uncomplicated, since few national borders were crossed en route to the port.

The second stream, from eastern Europe, followed a northern route across Russia to the Baltic Sea ports or across Germany to ports on the North Sea—Hamburg, Bremen, Rotterdam and Antwerp. Those from Russia, Poland and the northern provinces of Austria-Hungary—Bohemians, Moravians and Silesians—who sailed from the North Sea ports passed through one of a system of 13 control points along the eastern borders of Germany. These were located wherever major railroads entered the country from the east. At these control points the travelers were often required to spend the night on benches and floors, or on their baggage, until the train was made up on the next day. These special emigrant trains, with fourth-class cars, traveled nonstop directly to the ports.

The pre-sailing period of waiting at the port might be short or long, for the train schedules were not linked with sailing dates. In most cities, both Atlantic and Mediterranean, some provision was always made for the care of emigrants who were forced to wait for ship accommodations. Usually this was paid for by the steamship companies, who were required by the governments to watch over the prospective passengers.

At most ports the travelers were housed in private boardinghouses. Those in Italy were strictly supervised by the authorities. The Hungarian government built and operated an emigrant hotel at Fiume.

But the best of all European port shelters was the Auswanderer Hallen near Hamburg, Germany, built and operated by the Hamburg-American Line, which carried more eastern European steerage passengers than any other company. This was a 40-building model city with a capacity of 4,000. On his arrival and before he was assigned accommodations, the traveler was examined by a physician and, if necessary, he was required to bathe and his clothes were fumigated. The average wait here was three days.

The most important activity on the dock before the emigrants boarded the ship (though occasionally this was done in a dining room or saloon before sailing) was answering a number of questions recorded on manifest lists. Manifests were prepared for all passengers, both steerage and cabin, on forms prescribed by the United States.

These manifests, first required by the 1893 immigration law, were sheets containing a maximum of 30 numbered names of passengers. Twenty-nine questions were listed at the top of the manifest sheet, and after each name a ship's officer wrote the answers (by numbers) to the questions.

The purpose of the answers was to offer a concise history of the incoming alien, containing all the information which could aid the American immigration officers in the enforcement of the law. Here is a typical example:

(1) Full name: *Litschky, Samuel;* (2) age: *32;* (3) sex: *male;* (4) whether single or married: *single;* (5) calling or occupation: *watchmaker;* (6) whether able to read or write: *yes;* (7) nationality (the country of which a citizen or subject): *Polish;* (8) race: *Hebrew;* (9) last permanent residence: *Warsaw, Poland;* (10) name and complete address of nearest relative or friend in country from which immigrant comes: *Moisse Chisznak, 67 Neminov, Warsaw, cousin;* (11) seaport of landing in the United States: *New York;* (12) final destination, if any, beyond port of landing: *Bridgeport, Connecticut;* (13) whether having a ticket through to such final destination: *yes;* (14)

whether an alien has paid his own passage, or whether it has been paid by any other person or by any corporation, society, municipality, or government, and, if so, by whom: *brother Jozef;* (15) whether in possession of thirty dollars: *$35;* (16) whether going to join a relative or friend and if so, what relative or friend, his name and the complete address: *Jozef Litschky, 287 Fairfield Avenue, Bridgeport, Connecticut;* (17) whether ever before in the United States and if so, when and where: *no;* (18) whether ever in prison or almshouse or an institution or hospital for the care and treatment of the insane or supported by charity: *no;* (19) whether a polygamist: *no;* (20) whether an anarchist: *no;* (21) whether coming by reason of any offer, solicitation, promise or agreement, expressed or implied, to perform labor in the United States: *no, though brother knows where he can find work in a jewelry store;* (22) general condition of health, mental and physical: *good;* (23) whether deformed or crippled: *neither;* (24) height: *five feet, five inches;* (25) weight: *158 pounds;* (26) complexion: *dark;* (27) color of hair and eyes: *brown, black;* (28) marks of identification: *scar, left shoulder, from a fall;* (29) place of birth: *Warsaw, Poland.*

To assure that the proper care and accuracy had been exercised in the preparation of manifests, the law required the master or first officer and the ship's surgeon (who had checked the medical questions) to take an oath before an American Consular Service officer as to the truth of the manifest information before sailing. A similar oath was sworn before an immigration officer at the port of arrival that the manifests were, to the best of their knowledge and belief, true, and that none of the aliens belonged to any of the excluded classes. A fine of $10 was imposed both for failure to list any alien and for the lack of complete information.

The second major procedure at the port of embarkation was the medical examination of passengers in accordance with a section of the immigration law of 1893. One of the items in this law placed the responsibility for the certification of the health of passengers squarely upon the steamship lines, and most seaport medical examinations were made by doctors employed by the companies, either the ship's doctor or a specially engaged physician. Some passengers were always rejected for health causes, but the examination was in most cases too rapid to disclose any but the most obvious defects and diseases.

An exception to this pattern was the pre-embarkation medical examination at Italian ports after 1908. It was conducted by doctors of the United States Marine Hospital Service (later the Public Health Service) attached to the local consulate. They reported their findings to the consul, who had the power either of authorizing or preventing a ship's departure.

Interestingly enough, this pre-sailing medical inspection at Italian ports evolved from the experience of Fiorello La Guardia while he was American consul at Fiume from 1903 to 1906, many years before he gained fame as a United States Congressman and as Mayor of New York City.

Fiume was the chief port of Hungary on the Adriatic Sea. One of La Guardia's main duties was to inspect departing emigrants in numbers up to 2,000 per boat. During his three years there he cleared about ninety thousand persons—Slavs and Magyars, Germans, Russians and Italians.

Most consuls carried out in routine or lax fashion the foreign service regulations requiring that they "certify to the health of all passengers and give the ship a certificate that it had cleared from port free from contagious diseases or illnesses subject to quarantine regulations." La Guardia, however, proved to be a conscientious Foreign Service officer; as America's only representative in Fiume he badgered the shipping companies into obedience to the letter, threatened them in cases of noncompliance and occasionally almost caused international incidents. His extraordinary sympathy for the emigrating peasants made him persistent. He bombarded the State Department with suggestions on spelling out the detailed routines necessary.

Later the Italians, realizing the value of the system as La Guardia had established it, asked for and received the assistance of the American health officers at their ports of embarkation, but the practice was not written into the immigration law until 1924.

Vaccination and the disinfection of baggage were routinely performed at ports of embarkation. The next health check would be in quarantine and finally on Ellis Island.

The steerage passengers entered the ship by a gangway near either the bow or the stern of the ship, depending on the location of their accommodations. Berths were sometimes assigned by manifest numbers. The available deck space was open and small, and the area was filled with winches, hatch covers and all sorts of maritime machinery.

Almost immediately the passengers were directed down deep stairways to any of two or three enclosed lower decks.

They were now in steerage. This was to be their virtual prison for most of the voyage. But whatever their first impressions, they were definitely on their way.

4

Voyage to the Future

steerage, n. . . . 2. (from its originally being located near the rudder): a section in a passenger ship for passengers paying the lowest fares and given inferior accommodations.

Webster's New International Dictionary, 3d ed.

Steerage! The very word still brings shudders to many older immigrants who went through Ellis Island in the first three decades of its operation.

Steerage was a unique phenomenon of American immigration in the periods of both sail and steam. The earliest American immigration laws in 1819, 1847 and 1848 concerned steerage conditions on sailing vessels, where the passenger mortality rate per voyage was about ten per cent. The government's attempts to improve the conditions continued unabated with the introduction of steamships and their crowding of steerage accommodations in order to gain the greatest possible profit. From the 1870s to 1925, the overcrowded and unsanitary conditions on many vessels amounted to a scandal; passengers were often treated more like animals than human beings.

The United States Immigration Commission (called the Dillingham Commission after the chairman, Senator Wil-

liam Dillingham of Vermont) devoted a good deal of attention to the steerage problem as a part of an exhaustive
study of the problem of the "new" immigrants ordered by
President Theodore Roosevelt in 1907. The Commission
formally established two types of steerage: the old-type or
old and the new-type or new. The former class predomi-
nated on the Mediterranean lines; the latter was found on
the better ships of the North Atlantic service. Some ships
were equipped with both types.

The findings of the Commission, published in 1911,
showed that conditions on many ships with old-type steerage were deplorable, and that the nightmare of the voyage
often formed an unhappy introduction to our country. As
the report stated, "The typical old-type steerage is the
poorest possible introduction to, and preparation for, American life. It inevitably lowers the standards of decency, even
of the immigrants, and too often breaks down their moral
and physical stamina. It shatters their bright visions of
American life, and lands them cynical and embittered. . . ."

The old-type steerage was described by a Commission
investigator who traveled on a westbound voyage from
Italy. "Imagine a large room, perhaps seven feet in height,"
he wrote in 1909, "extending the entire breadth of the ship
and about one-third of its length, located for the most part
in the bow or stern (fore or aft) sections. The floor and
ceilings are sometimes of iron, but more often of wood.
Through the center of the room, very probably, descends
the shaft to the hold.

"This room is filled with a framework of iron pipes,
forming a double tier of six-by-two-feet berths, with only
sufficient space left to serve as aisles or passageways. . . .
Such a compartment will sometimes accommodate as many

as three hundred passengers and is duplicated in other parts of the ship and on other decks.

"The open deck space reserved for steerage passengers is usually very limited, and situated in the worst part of the ship, subject to the most violent motion, to the dirt from the stacks and the odors from the hold and galleys. . . . The only provisions for eating are frequently shelves or benches or along the sides or in the passages of sleeping compartments. Dining rooms are rare and if found are often shared with berths installed along the walls. Toilets and washrooms are completely inadequate; salt water only is available.

"The ventilation is almost always inadequate, and the air soon becomes foul. The unattended vomit of the seasick, the odors of not too clean bodies, the reek of food and the awful stench of the nearby toilet rooms make the atmosphere of the steerage such that it is a marvel that human flesh can endure it. . . . Most immigrants lie in their berths for most of the voyage, in a stupor caused by the foul air. The food often repels them. . . . It is almost impossible to keep personally clean. All of these conditions are naturally aggravated by the crowding. . . ."

The typical steerage of the immigrant boats so affected some of those who had endured its hardships and horrors that they wrote extensively about it. Jacob Riis, a Danish journalist and social worker who passed through Castle Garden in 1870, told his story in *The Making of an American* (1901). Mary Antin, a Russian writer who arrived at Boston in 1894, wrote *The Promised Land* (1912). Journalists posed as immigrants in order to observe and expose conditions.

Edward Steiner, an 1891 immigrant from central Europe, became a clergyman in Iowa, but devoted himself to studying the problems of immigrants. He made many trips on the various routes and in the two steerage types. This is his comment on the old-type, from his *On the Trail of the Immigrant,* published in 1906.

"The steerage never changes, neither its location nor its furnishings. It lies over the stirring screws, sleeps to the staccato of trembling steel railings and hawsers. Narrow, steep and slippery stairways lead to it.

"Crowds everywhere, ill smelling bunks, uninviting washrooms—this is steerage. The odors of scattered orange peelings, tobacco, garlic and disinfectants meeting but not blending. No lounges or chairs for comfort, and a continual babel of tongues—this is steerage."

Even in the early 1890s there were a few steamships which pioneered in the new-type steerage. The first adequate description of such steerage was a slim volume by Robert Louis Stevenson titled *The Amateur Immigrant,* published in 1895. Traveling to New York from Glasgow as a second-cabin passenger in a British vessel, he passed most of his time in the steerage. Stevenson was a keen observer who made friends easily, and his narrative presents an excellent picture of new-type accommodations.

Investigators of the Dillingham Commission in 1910 hailed the improvements which had been made. "The new-type steerage is a modified second cabin, with simpler and plainer accommodations," its report stated. "Separate staterooms are provided, having from two to eight berths in each. Sanitary conditions are better than in the old-type, but the lack of ventilation still exists. . . . At least the crowding is eliminated, food is served in dining rooms and the sum total is more contributory to recognizing human dignity."

Between 1900 and 1910 the new type came to be a feature of some of the boats on the North Atlantic route, but most immigrants still made the trip in the crowded and unsanitary traditional steerage.

Greek Teodor Makropoulos, now in his late seventies, was able to refresh the memory of his 1905 trip, when he was seventeen, by consulting his worn diary, for he "knew the trip would be something I would never forget, something I would want to tell my children and grandchildren about, and therefore I would want to put it all down."

Mr. Makropoulos sailed from Piraeus, the port of Athens, on an English liner in which, from his story, the steerage was obviously old-type. He paid $36 for the 15-day voyage; and the ship made stops at Fiume on the Adriatic and at Naples, so that the steerage finally held over two thousand. His fellow passengers were other Greeks, Syrians, Croatians, Dalmatians, Carpathians and Italians.

The steerage was located in the stern and forward sections of the ship on four levels, many of them below the water line. One lower deck was devoted entirely to steerage compartments.

"The rooms had about 150 people in each one, sometimes more," he recalled. "Our bunks were upper and lower and we had no place to put our bags, so we had to hold them on the mattress like we were sleeping with them and it was not very comfortable. We did not have springs, but instead there was some kind of metal strips which we could feel through the mattress. It was a great big burlap bag of straw, and not very much of that either. Besides, it smelled because a lot of people had probably been seasick on it and I am sure it had never been washed.

"There were no pillows and we used our life preservers instead. They were hard cork, I think, and so I put my folded coat over mine. I had a thin blanket, but it was never cold so I did not need it. Everybody slept in their clothes. There was no fresh air and after about three days the smell was terrible.

"To make it worse, in good weather everyone wanted to be on the decks at both ends of the boat and the space was little, and most of us had to stand up in a close crowd in order to get some fresh air.

"We had three stormy days . . . so we just stayed in our berths and everyone was sick, and no one came to clean up. We did not even have any pails or cans and once in a while there would be some sawdust put on the floor. I don't believe I have ever felt worse in my life. It was the first time I was away from home and I was more homesick than seasick.

"Oh yes, we each had a plate and a cup and a spoon, and we ate in our berths. The cooks came with big pots of soup and stew and filled our dishes, but most people did not even try to eat. We had to wash our things in the salt water in the same basin where we washed our faces and hands.

"Complain? Who would I complain to? And what would be the good? We were just trapped, that's all, and I was never as happy in my life as when we got to New York and Ellis Island!"

The old-type steerage pattern occasionally had some variations. An Italian named Guido Gallucci made the trip from Naples in 1907, when the immigration to the

United States from Italy was at its peak. He paid $36. His sister was with him and they were to join his parents, who had immigrated three years before and sent them tickets.

The unique feature of this voyage was that he and about 150 others shared their steerage quarters with a race horse! (Newspaper stories the day after the boat's arrival verify Guido's story, for complaints had been lodged with the Ellis Island authorities.)

"When we went on board in the morning my sister Carmela had to go to a special ladies' section and I to one for men only," said Guido. "We were almost all Neapolitans from central Italy. About three hundred men were usually in the section I was in, but this was cut in half for this particular trip. The double bunks were along the walls and in rows towards the center, with only small aisles between.

"But in the middle of the room, where some bunks had been taken away, there was a closed stall about four feet high and in it was a horse! Some of the men asked a sailor if there was not some mistake, that maybe the horse should be with the freight but not with people. But no, this animal belonged to a rich American who was in first class and this was the only place they could find room for him. All this was very puzzling because most Italian ships have a government representative on board as the law required. There was such a man but he seemed to think it was a great joke, so I guess he must have been paid to allow it.

"So the horse was with us while we slept and while we ate. He was a nervous horse, and he stomped a lot and neighed and made funny noises all the time except when it was dark. There was a man who did nothing but take care of that horse and twice a day he would take it up the stairs with boards over the steps, and the horse would get his exercise. The people on deck were as astounded as we were! Nobody said a word because the horse was kept clean, and as a matter of fact it was something to talk about! Besides, the ship was crowded and where could we go?

"We had no dining room and we ate wherever we could find room—in our bunks, on deck, on the stairways, everywhere and anywhere. There were no chairs at all any place and so we sometimes sat on the floor to eat.

"When we went on board we passed a storeroom and were given a blanket in which we found a tin pan, a dipper type of cup, a spoon and a fork, but no knife. I guess that was because many people tore the meat apart with their hands. The man told us that we had to keep these for the trip. We washed them in a barrel of cold sea water and with all the greasy pasta dishes it was not very good.

"We each had a red card which said 'Good for one ration' and an officer told us to organize in groups of six and appoint a *capo di rancio* [rations chief] who would go to the galley at each meal, hand over the tickets and bring back whatever we were to have, also the wine to go with it. Then he would come back and serve us. Mostly we had macaroni soup, at least so often that that's all I remember. One day I was the *capo*—we took turns—and we had biscuits, and the steward took them out of a dirty burlap sack.

"I was used to washing regularly but we had to wait in line for a basin, sometimes for half an hour, and of course this was before the days of showers. The water was not even fresh; it was salt and some people got skin infections and split lips from the dried salt.

"One thing I did not understand. I never saw my sister during the trip because the people in different compartments went on deck at different times and then had to go back inside to make room for others. I did not sleep well on this trip. There were too many people around all the time and that horse really bothered me! Ellis Island seemed like paradise when I got there."

Bernard Lewandowski was one of the more fortunate passengers traveling in a North Atlantic vessel in the new-type steerage. He has only pleasant memories of his voyage in 1897.

"When I heard the stories of others on crowded boats," Mr. Lewandowski said, "I knew I had been very lucky to have come on a German boat, the *Kaiser Wilhelm*. If I remember right, my father—I was only thirteen but I remember almost everything, really I do—paid a little more because it was a fast boat and it had just made some sort of a speed record." (He was correct. In 1897 the liner had crossed from Southampton to New York, the nonstop part of the voyage from Hamburg, in 5 days and 15 hours.) "My father used to say that was the best money he had ever spent—the difference between other boats and our fast one. For one thing we had portholes, for we were above the water line and except during rough weather we could open them and air our section. It was the family section and we had berths on two levels, upper and lower, together in a partitioned space, not out in the open like most.

"Our mattresses were of bagging filled with straw which they said was burned after each round trip. If I close my eyes I can still smell it, believe me, because there is nothing in the world fresher. After we were in New York on the Lower East Side, we had mattresses stuffed with shavings, then with feathers, and they were not the same.

"The sections were whitewashed, and the hallways were washed every day. The blankets—we each had one—were clean and fresh, and we each had a pillow filled with fresh straw, too. On some boats they had no pillows. So I am sure from the stories I have heard that our trip was not like many others."

Though many official investigations exposed the evils of the steerage system, the resulting legislation (see Chapter 11) was not necessarily obeyed by foreign steamship lines because such laws were apparently difficult if not impossible to enforce. Prosecution was time-consuming, and the stated penalties, if imposed, were negligible in comparison with the income enjoyed by the steamship companies.

The monotony of the voyage was officially broken twice. The ship's doctor visited each compartment in a hurried survey; this was to avoid a fine if sickness was not later reported to immigration officials. Finally, on the last day, all passports were routinely checked.

In spite of the miserable conditions, all was not gloom in steerage. There were constant card games, much music and occasional dancing. And the conversation about the future was endless.

Rumors circulated about Ellis Island; the stories of rejections and deportations were repeated endlessly. Those who were familiar with the routines drilled the novices in giving the right answers which would prevent delays and difficulties. Scores of what one investigator called "useless lies" were rehearsed over and over. "Many persons whose entry into the country would be in no way hindered by even the strictest enforcement of the letter of the immigration laws," he reported, "were trembling in their shoes and preparing to evade or defeat the purpose of questions which they had heard would be put to them."

Men were coached in two important areas: "Remember, you have no work, and you paid your own way." The first was to avoid possible difficulties under the anti-contract labor laws (see Chapter 8), the last to convince the officer that there was no possibility that the immigrant would not be able to make a living and thus become a "public charge."

Many passengers began learning and practicing a few English words, phrases and sentences. The end of the voyage would result in the clearance process and, if successful, the immigrant would need some knowledge of English to make his way in the fabulous new life of opportunities which he was sure awaited him.

The decline of mass immigration to the United States from Europe dealt the death blow to steerage. Immediately following the introduction of the quota and "national origin" laws in the early 1920s the steamship companies found that the long-time traditional steerage, which was planned to pack together as many passengers as could be squeezed into the less desirable portions of a ship, was no longer practicable or profitable.

The thousands upon thousands of immigrants clamoring for space had become a mere trickle. Whereas steerage was often sold out a year in advance throughout 1920, the steerage sections of vessels were almost empty by 1924, when the last of the restrictive laws became operative.

The issuance of visas by American consuls abroad tended to exclude newcomers, as the law intended. The type of immigrant changed. After the postwar labor boom the demand for unskilled laborers lessened, and the world-wide depression resulted in an excess of emigrants over immigrants for the first time in American history. Those who arrived were members of the middle class who could afford to pay for better accommodations.

On passenger ships the former steerage was superseded by tourist or third class, with four- or six-passenger state-rooms replacing the huge compartments filled with bunks.

The traditional steerage and all it signified were to be recalled as one of the grim and shameful aspects of the immigration story.

5

First Encounter with the New World

By the time the sea voyage was approaching its end most steerage passengers were in a state of bewilderment. The physical confinement in crowded and ill-ventilated quarters below the water line, or in the bow area, where every plunge of the ship was felt, or in the stern over the screw propeller, where every turn of the shaft caused vibration, usually proved nerve-wracking.

Almost all European emigrants suffered from what today would be called a psychic shock or an emotional upset brought on by the termination of everything which represented the familiar past. The happy hopes for a better future—the principal reason for departure—were based on hearsay and the stories which had been sent back by relatives, friends or compatriots who had apparently found happiness in their new country. Many of the tales seemed too good to be true.

The trips to the European port of embarkation were often long and tiring, and the physical and emotional let-down during the voyage inevitable. Its long-awaited end was the single-minded goal of each passenger.

Among the older people interviewed by the author in a New York rest home for Italians was Signora Bianca De Carli, a 78-year-old widow who had made the voyage from Genoa in 1913, when almost 900,000 aliens, a quarter of a million of whom were of her nationality, passed through the Port of New York. Like other oldsters interviewed, she apparently remembered every detail of her trip to America 53 years earlier with her husband Antonio and their three children.

She spoke of her feelings as she approached America and realized that her new life was soon to begin:

"Sir, you cannot understand—only those of us left who passed through the Island can speak of it knowingly. We were impatient but yet patient; we were nervous—how do you say, confused, *agitato?*—because we still were not sure of passing through. A thousand times during the last day or two I put my hands on my passport and papers which I kept wrapped in a handkerchief under the front of my dress. This was just to make sure they were still there.

"One of my companions said, 'Signora, you are very foolish! When you keep your hand inside your dress and on your breast you are telling everyone that your papers and money are there! Maybe a bad person will see. Take your hands away. Nothing can happen now.'

"Now, years later, I know it was very foolish and silly, but we heard so many stories about others who were turned back because their papers were not in order. Everyone asked each other over and over, 'Are your papers in order?' and then we always checked them. No one trusted their pockets even, because this showed where our money was, and crowded together most of the time it would be easy to have our pockets picked.

"One woman had sewed her papers and money (in small bills which she planned to cash in at the Island) into the folds of her seventeen skirts! Yes, seventeen; I know I am right in remembering, and she wore them all. She came from a Hungarian or something province which is no more, and she told me that a woman's wealth was proved by the number of skirts she could wear.

"Well, that afternoon when we could see the land (it was the south shore of Long Island) a steamship man told us all to check our papers, as if we hadn't done this thousands of times, and have everything ready so that it would not be necessary to search through our bags and bundles. He told us to have our money ready to show, which was one of the questions we had answered, including the head tax (I remember it was $4 because we had the $8 set aside in lire) and what we would exchange for railroad tickets if we were going beyond New York.

"Well, this skirt lady I was telling you about started to cry and wail. We finally knew that she thought she would not have time to cut the hundreds of threads which held those little paper monies into her skirts. Another lady had a lot of sewing scissors and a little blade, and so about five of us divided the skirts and we went over every inch of them —they had lots of folds and when spread out were very wide—and put what we found each in a little pile.

"She even had love letters which she wanted to be safe. When she was sure that no one in America cared how many skirts she had, each with its money, she wore only two through the examinations and carried the others in a big bundle!

"Yes, we all trembled because of the strangeness and the confusion and the unknownness. Some were weak from no movement and exercise, and some were sick because of the smells and the unfresh air. But somehow this did not matter because we now knew it was almost over. But I will never forget it!"

A Polish arrival in the peak year of 1907, Mrs. Zedlinka Wojciechowski, then 22, recalled the last day of the voyage nearly sixty years later.

"We had had a bad trip, huge waves and the ship plunging around so much that for six of the nine-day trip we could not even go on deck for a little fresh air. This was the only time I could meet my husband, who was with the men, and I felt very lonely and lost. All the portholes in the upper steerage were closed and I felt as if I would smother if the trip would not soon end.

"Then early one morning it was calm and the engines, which were so close underneath us that the regular sound was all the time present, stopped and it was like a dead silence. We could not, of course, see out much and all kinds of stories started up. Most agreed that we were near America and that the hour we had waited for was now.

"Soon a steward came and told us we could go on the deck because they wanted to clean and air the cabins before we reached quarantine—I think there was a bad disease in Europe and they wanted no one to have it because everyone would then have to stay on the ship. Quarantine, he said, was the first part of our landing, and when he gave the signal we should come back and make ourselves look as nice as possible so that we would be welcome. He said this in German—it was a German boat from Hamburg and there were over nine hundred in steerage, and only three hundred upstairs—that was first and second class. I understood because I know Yiddish, but many did not and we tried to tell them why they should get clean and nice for our reception.

"The slowdown was to let the pilot come on board from his boat. We were all crowded together and packed in the little open space in the rear. Only a few could stand by the railing and they were lucky. But right after we started again —it was now calm with just a little swell—people started shouting and pointing to the right. It was land far off!

"At first it looked just like a line, but by noon it was clear. This was our first sight of America, the shore of Long Island. Some broke into tears, but they were, you must understand, happy tears. Some of the women wailed and keened and would not stop even when we were all so very happy. It was their tiredness, I suppose. The people at the railings held their places and others started to bring their bundles and bags to the deck, making it more crowded. Now all we had to do was wait. But even the sight of the shore far away meant the end of a long time of planning and worry.

"My husband and I did not just plan to come one day and leave the next, not at all. We applied for our exit papers and waited. We had made a deposit to the agent for our boat tickets even though we did not know when we could leave. Lots of our fellows received tickets from their relatives in America, but we had only the letter of a friend from our village who said we could use his address in New York City and he would take care of us.

"When the time came after six months of waiting, we had to break up our home and get rid of everything except what we could carry. I took my baby chair—it was so little and I filled it with clothing and wrapped it in a blanket—but they took it away from me at Hamburg. But before that there was the long railroad trip across Germany with many stops for inspections, more inspections and changes to the side switches where we waited and waited, for it was an 'emigrant train' and even the freight trains passed us. When we arrived in Hamburg we had to wait for a boat for five more days, though the hotels of the steamship company were clean and comfortable. Watching the European shore disappear was another shock because it was final that we were on our way and we could no longer turn back. Then the long trip with no air and the separation and the noise of the engines and the up-and-down, side-to-side movements did not make us feel very happy. And when we saw the land of the United States we felt relief and knew that our new life was very near. It was like the doctor had given us a dose of happiness."

The harbor pilots boarded incoming ships from the Ambrose Lightship stationed in Ambrose Channel, the entrance to the Lower Bay of New York Harbor. This is between Coney Island in New York State and Sandy Hook in New Jersey. The southern part of the Lower Bay was the quarantine area, where all ships entering the harbor were required to stop.

The Port of New York was officially open only from

7 A.M. to 8:30 P.M. No steamers were allowed to enter the harbor outside of these hours except by special permit. The ships were examined at quarantine from 7 A.M. to 5 P.M., and later only by special arrangement. Most vessels arriving after five o'clock anchored for the night; they were often scattered in irregular lines throughout the quarantine area awaiting their turns the next morning.

The term "quarantine" referred to the period in which an incoming ship's cabin passengers were inspected for possible contagious diseases—scarlet fever, measles and diphtheria—and more particularly the five so-called epidemic diseases: cholera, plague, smallpox, typhus (typhoid fever) and yellow fever. The medical inspection was conducted jointly by New York State health authorities and federal health officers until 1921, when all quarantine activities of the Port of New York were put under the sole control of the United States Public Health Service.

This examination of cabin class passengers at quarantine was the counterpart of the later inspection of steerage passengers at Ellis Island. United States citizens were exempted, but all aliens, both visitors and immigrants, in both first and second class, passed by in single file and were quickly checked by the doctors who had boarded the vessel. A very few were marked to be sent to Ellis Island for more complete examinations. For example, of 100,000 cabin passengers arriving in New York during 1905, only 3,000 were required to pass through the Island; during this same year the steerage passengers inspected there numbered 800,000.

Afterwards, the medical officers met with the ship's surgeon, who reported any cases of sickness among passengers of all classes during the voyage. Many cases of measles and other children's diseases were always contracted during a trip. Those in the ship's hospital were transferred immediately by cutter to Ellis Island. This was the only possible point of contact between steerage passengers and federal officials at quarantine.

On two occasions serious outbreaks of epidemic diseases —cholera in 1892 and typhus in 1920 and 1921—were discovered among steerage passengers and they were removed to isolation wards, first at Hoffman Island in the harbor, then to the Ellis Island hospital.

During the medical inspection the immigration inspector examined the manifests for the aliens in both cabin classes and asked a few routine nonmedical questions, sending a few to Ellis Island for further questioning.

For most steerage passengers the time at quarantine was only a period of waiting, and their impatience and irritation was very great. To pass the time some would attempt to recognize waiting relatives and friends who might be in the sizable groups which collected on the Brooklyn shore at Gravesend Bay. Through binoculars, these waiting throngs a half-mile away tried to identify and wave to those on the anchored ships whom they would be meeting later.

Soon after the visiting inspectors had dispatched the detained and sick passengers to Ellis Island and had climbed down the ladders to their waiting cutter, the ship moved north through The Narrows leading to Upper New York Bay. Many an immigrant's heart beat faster, for the rural shorelines on either side soon gave way to the harbor itself.

The Narrows, between Brooklyn and Staten Island, is less than a mile in width at its narrowest point. As the boat steamed slowly through this passage, the harbor, with the tip of Manhattan Island a mere six miles away, came into view in what is generally considered one of the most spectacular sights in the world. Even today the most sophisticated modern traveler never fails to be impressed. The newcomers from the Old World arriving during the 1890s and the first two decades of the twentieth century were overwhelmed.

The first object of every pair of eyes was the Statue of Liberty. Every one of the elderly ex-immigrants with whom the author talked invariably lingered tenderly on the first impression made by the statue. "Mein Gott, what a grosse frau she was! I thought she was one of the seven wonders of the world," said a German nearing his eightieth birthday. An Italian merely murmured over and over, "Bella, bella, oh, bella."

A Hungarian explained the spell of the colossus: "No one had ever before or after seen its like. We were crowded on the front and the back lower decks, all turned in one direction where lay our futures. Here was this huge lady stretching the torch of freedom into the sky and we knew what it meant. This was why we were there at that moment in that spot with Ellis Island just beyond. It was the most beautiful sight of my many years!"

A Russian Jew who had escaped a pogrom in his native village paid this tribute: "Freedom is easy nowadays. Everyone has it and no one worries about it. But when I arrived in this wonderful country I felt as if I had a new life before me. I *knew* it, and it was proved true. But the statue greeted me as a friend. The big tablet she carried was like that of Moses, who led the chosen people out of bondage. Her torch was later lighted at night but *we* knew the light was there all the time."

A Polish man said: "The bigness of Mrs. Liberty overcame us. No one spoke a word, for she was like a goddess and we knew she represented the big, powerful country which was to be our future home."

Just beyond the statue was Ellis Island, about half a mile to the northwest. The sight of their final destination warmed the hearts of the observers. Then the buildings a mile away on the lower tip of Manhattan Island came clearly into view.

Beyond the open space of the Battery, with the circular Castle Garden, the former immigration station, near the water, the tall buildings of from 10 to 25 stories seemed to be packed solidly to form a background. The immigrants could only stare in amazement. The majority of them had probably never before seen a building of more than several stories, if that.

Both sides of Broadway were lined with towers, and the two highest, the 47-floor Singer Building (1908) and the 60-floor Woolworth Building (1913) were particularly awesome. These impressive structures caused the newcomers to stare with mouths agape at the majesty and wonder of this, their promised land.

The ships made their way up the Hudson River to their piers, mainly on the New York shore, though lines carrying about a third of the arrivals docked at Hoboken and Jersey City.

The privileged passengers of the first and second cabin,

and any United States citizens in steerage, for whom no inspection was required, disembarked onto the pier to pass customs and have their baggage and passports checked. They were often met by happy and eager friends.

The steerage passengers were greeted by no one, for they still faced their greatest test, the clearance process at Ellis Island.

The policy of inspecting only cabin class passengers at quarantine and requiring all foreign steerage passengers, both visitors and immigrants, to pass through Ellis Island was a carryover from the period of state supervision at Castle Garden. Strangely enough, this practice was seldom directly challenged as discriminatory and undemocratic, although immigration authorities continually called attention to the numbers of undesirable aliens who avoided detailed questioning and physical examination by traveling in the cabin classes.

The Island medical examination was approved as necessary, but no one questioned the screening process from the standpoint of both social justice and fairness as well as the uniform application of the immigration laws to all aliens.

Immigrants who could afford the more expensive second and first class accommodations, therefore, supposedly formed an elite. Many immigrants who had attained financial success in the United States purchased cabin class accommodations for their parents so that the trip would be comfortable and the detention at Ellis Island could be avoided.

The segregation and special treatment of the steerage passengers undeniably colored all the discussion of immigration restriction by encouraging the impression that steerage passengers of the "new" immigration were little more than barbarians.

After the ship had docked and while the cabin passengers were disembarking, the steerage passengers left the ship by a gangplank near the stern and poured across the pier to a large reserved space at the end. Each wore in a conspicuous place a tag with his name and, in large figures, his manifest number, which was to form his identification during the processing at Ellis Island.

The tag of our prototype immigrant of Chapter 3, for example, would have read

SAMUEL LITSCHKY
M 15

meaning that he was number 15 in the M manifest group. At the designated pier space the aliens assembled in groups of 30 according to the manifest letters under which they were listed.

The heavier and bulkier luggage was meanwhile loaded on the barges or small sidewheelers rented under contract by the steamship company to transfer the steerage passengers to Ellis Island. The responsibility of the firms ended only when all steerage passengers had passed through the Island; the companies paid for any meals served and for the expenses of any passenger detained on the Island for reasons other than sickness.

The lower enclosed decks of the barges were filled with the mountains of baggage, while the passengers were packed on the top decks, open on the sides above the railings. The manifests for all the passengers on a ship were sent to the

Island with the first load. The barges often made several trips from the pier to the Island in order to deliver all the immigrants who were on a ship.

On arrival at the Island's landing slip, the barge attendants directed the passengers, by manifest groups, to the large Main Building. This was the reception building through which every arriving steerage immigrant was processed and through which 16 million newcomers to the United States eventually passed.

The long journey was nearing its end.

6

On the Threshold

An observer in 1911 vividly and sympathetically described the behavior of a typical manifest group on its way to the Island. "The immigrants are in a constant turmoil of excitement until they board the ferryboats on the last lap of their journeys. To them Ellis Island is a complicated labyrinth leading to freedom. Their stolid faces hide frightened, throbbing hearts. They obey the signs, gestures and directions of the attendants as dumbly as cattle, and as patiently."

The average newcomer was burdened with handicaps which increased his dread of the imminent inspection process. He was first of all a stranger who could not speak English; his own language was often not even the same as that of many of his companions on the manifest list. He was of rural birth, with a background of poverty. He might be uneducated, or sometimes illiterate. He had rarely before been required to meet confusing and unfamiliar situations.

Debarkation from the barges was not always immediate. When a ship carrying a thousand steerage passengers arrived in port simultaneously with several others, the race to land them on the Island as soon as possible resulted in many loaded transfer boats moored along the quay at the Island. Later arrivals were often held on board for an hour or two, and sometimes many hours.

The effect of this detention when the long-awaited objective was so near and yet so far was described by Karel Novotny, a Hungarian arrival in 1912, as the most vexing of all the many annoyances he had suffered. "I may have just been the victim of a lot of bad luck," he said, "but even then the most patient of men will reach the end."

To begin with, Karel had failed to obtain a visa for Belgium, from which he was to sail. The boat left Antwerp without him. "I had to wait several days for accommodations, and even then my berth was in a dining room—that is, a lot of rough wooden tables with benches—which was also the only place except on the small rear deck where steerage passengers could relax and get away from the smelly quarters below the deck. We had good ventilation but always there were people and the smells of food. This increased our impatience to set foot on American land.

"When we arrived in New York we had to stay overnight on the ship at the dock and they would not even let us go on deck for fear, I guess, that someone would jump off. In the morning we went onto the dock, but something was wrong. The little boat did not come, and it was the middle of the afternoon when we started for Ellis Island.

"We got there at about four o'clock, but there were about five or six other crowded boats ahead of us and there was no promise of when we could go ashore. Now it was not our fault that we were late. A man in uniform came out from the big building with another man who had a round thing which he held to his mouth and into which he shouted [a megaphone]. In about four or five different languages he told us to be patient, that we would get off in a few hours when our turn came. Did we have any questions?

"Everyone shouted at once and there was a lot of noise. He said we would stay overnight on the Island and the steamship company would pay if we could not go through that day. Then we would be the first ones in the morning. Next some people asked how their relatives and friends, who were probably nearby waiting, would know about us and he said they would be told to come back.

"The babies were crying and screaming, and everyone was shouting and shaking their fists at the guards. Some boys and young men jumped off the upper deck on the big high piles and then to the cement walk beyond, but three guards grabbed them and made them jump back to the boat.

"When it got dark we knew we were stuck because there was still another boat before ours. Meanwhile we had seen a lot of people leaving the Island on the New York ferry-boat, and some of us recognized our friends and relatives. Such yelling and sobbing you never heard! Everyone was trying to send messages for the little moment that the two ships were near each other, and people waved handker-chiefs and felt better because they would see each other in the morning.

"We were all hungry because the steamship people did not pay for any food, and by that time those that had had some food with them had eaten almost all of it. When it was quite dark and the lights were shining through the windows nothing had yet happened. Some of the passengers began yelling and they grabbed the sailors and tried to force them to put down the gangplank. A lot of guards came out of the big building and yelled for us to be quiet. They were very angry and the people who understood English said they swore a lot and called us names. Some of the people threw orange peelings and banana skins at them and then started to throw out the life preservers that were in the racks.

"The man with the horn then came out and said he was sorry but we would have to stay overnight. We should hang on to our number cards and gather together by the letters, then go ashore and follow the guards. This we did in much confusion because everyone carried some bags and bundles. Our heavy luggage on the lower deck was to be taken to the baggage room.

"The dormitories were at least clean and the beds nice—I remember that the springs were really wonderful after the rope ones on the boat. After a little while we went to the restaurant, which was all white tile and clean. We could sit for our meal of good soup and two sandwiches. I remember one was ham. The steamship company paid for this and for our breakfast.

"The next morning bright and early we went through the inspection but lots of us had to wait for the ferryboats bringing those who were to meet us. Some of the people were still really raving mad and they muttered against the United States and the government, saying they would complain to the President. But most of us were just glad it was all over and there would be no more troubles."

In other situations when inspections were completed after dark and the staff was working in shifts, the immigrants were held overnight at government expense for their own safety and comfort, so that they would not be cast adrift, as it were, at the Battery ferry terminal or have to wait in railroad terminals, since practically no trains departed in the late evening hours.

When the flow into the Island was operating smoothly the processing might take as little as 45 minutes and seldom longer than three or four hours. At such times the immigrants disembarked immediately. On the landing they were formed in groups according to the manifest letter. There was much temporary confusion and shouting back and forth while everybody lined up under the direction of a guard. Most immigrants showed respect for the uniforms and obeyed instructions promptly.

During the early years of the Island, the aliens arrived dressed in their native costumes. Though a single nationality might be in the majority in a manifest group, there was always a varied mixture. The Hungarians were readily identified by their rough jackets and top boots. The Rumanians at all times and in all seasons wore long sheepskin coats. Russian men wore Cossack hats of fur or lambskin. Possibly two-thirds of the men had beards or mustaches; only the very young were clean shaven.

The women added touches of color to the scene, for without exception the men wore their best black suits for this memorable occasion. The common feature of all female clothing was the head kerchief, universally called the babushka.

The shawl was another standard piece of women's clothing; very likely it was of wool and was hand-knitted. Many of the women also wore aprons. Their feet, when they were not bare, might be in felt slippers or in boots. And, as one immigrant remembers, "the baby in arms was so common that it was almost like a part of the costume."

By 1912 such picturesque dress had become rare. It has been suggested that photographs received from relatives in the United States had produced a feeling of self-consciousness; the desire to "look American" caused many an immigrant to leave his native garb behind and set out dressed as inconspicuously as possible.

The other spectacle presented by the arrivals was the hand baggage they carried: bundles, baskets and bags of all types. Battered cases, bulging so much that they would not shut, were tied with rope. Some of the leather, cardboard and canvas bags seemed to be falling to bits, and straw baskets of every sort were fairly bursting.

But the most common type of baggage was the bundle; two out of three immigrants carried over their shoulders these packages of various sizes containing their most prized possessions. Some were of heavy burlap, others were gunny sacks of jute and hemp. Others were sheets, blankets or tablecloths with the ends knotted. The stronger and older the bearer, the bigger was the bundle. Some of the women exhibited a great deal of skill by carrying both babies and bundles in a precarious balance. A few walked calmly with huge bundles balanced on their heads.

All but the very young children were burdened with bags and bundles, usually gauged to their size and strength. None were empty-handed, for there were no porters and redcaps available on the Island, as there were on the piers. Even had there been, they would have found no customers among these heavy-laden travelers, who were accustomed to fend for themselves. This hand baggage, no matter what bulk or size, was carried through the entire inspection process.

What did the newcomers bring with them? Very little clothing, for the probable reason that they wanted to discard their old-style clothes just as they were casting off their former lives. What they brought were mementos of their past, many of no value except in their personal associations.

Always there were framed pictures of those left behind, religious objects, a few beloved books (if the owners could read), and small pieces of furniture often belonging to the children and carried by them. The womenfolk brought sentimental knickknacks and, because they could not be shipped without the danger of breakage, sets of dishes, bowls, vases and the like.

A large number of bundles contained kitchenware, even teakettles and pots and pans. Any tableware, whether silver plated, copper, pewter, or even tin, was brought along. In spite of their bulk, many a comforter, mattress or pillow was carried in an oversize bundle.

An Irishman would find room for a pot of shamrock; an Italian might bring in a cutting from the vineyard in his homeland. A bag of native soil was often brought along, for most of them came from rural areas and were lovers of the land.

Italians burdened themselves with wine, fruit, olive oil, nuts and even cheese. Greeks carried figs and olives. The Middle Europeans preferred their special kinds of sausages; many fellow passengers in steerage complained of the odors.

At the end of the landing ramp and just under the glass-covered walk leading to the main building an interpreter, the first of several an immigrant would meet in his progress through the Island, joined the guard to give the assembling groups simple directions in the necessary languages and to call out the numbers of the particular manifest group.

In many ways the interpreter was the most important cog in the inspection machinery. His was the most personal of the contacts the newcomer made on Ellis Island, and his responsibilities involved more than the translating of words. The meanings in the particular situation and question were often crucial in the determination of the immigrant's future. Only by the interpreter's patience and skill could the frequently indefinite and confused answers to the questions of the examining officers be clarified.

Ellis Island was always a linguist's paradise. Notices were posted in nine different languages—English, German, Greek, Hebrew, Italian, Magyar (Hungarian), Polish, Russian and Scandinavian (usually Swedish)—representing the major arriving nationalities of both the "old" and "new" immigration. Other languages might be added when conditions in Europe brought in large numbers of a specific nationality which had hitherto had limited representation.

Regardless of the port of departure, many languages were spoken by the immigrants arriving in a particular ship. For example, ships leaving from English ports invariably carried in steerage many Russian, Polish, Lithuanian, Finnish, Norwegian and Swedish emigrants who had reached England through the nearer Baltic Sea ports.

The Island's staff interpreters were so gifted multilingually that among those on duty at a particular time someone who spoke a particular language could always be located. The average number of languages spoken by an interpreter was said to have been six, but a dozen languages (including dialects almost like separate languages) were not uncommon. The record was 15.

The interpreters were selected by qualifying federal civil service examinations in their major specialties. Many of the linguists were old-timers from Castle Garden years. Some were themselves immigrants who had gained their fluency before emigrating.

The interpreter who was later to become nationally famous in American public life was Fiorello La Guardia. After his maverick activities as Consular Agent at Fiume, Hungary (see Chapter 3), La Guardia was disenchanted and frustrated. So in 1906 he resigned from the Foreign Service and returned to the United States. After a number of menial and underpaid jobs he realized that he should make use of the language skills he had acquired in his Foreign Service posts at Budapest, Trieste and Fiume. Besides his native Italian, he had learned to speak German, Yiddish, French, Hungarian and Croatian.

After he had passed the examination for interpreter, his name was placed high on the eligible list because of a fairly recent increased influx of Croats and Serbians. His appointment with an annual salary of $1,200 permitted him to attend night school at the New York University Law School, after a full day's work on Ellis Island.

The two-year period (1908-1910) when La Guardia worked at the Island marked the crest of the tide of "new" immigrants. As many as 5,000 passed through daily. In his posthumously published autobiography, *The Making of an Insurgent,* he told of his work with the newcomers.

"I never managed during the years I worked there," he wrote, "to become callous to the mental anguish, the disappointment and the despair I witnessed almost daily. . . . At best the work was an ordeal." But his basic sympathy for the underdog enabled him to make his job more than a mere succession of highly practiced routines unemotionally performed. On the Island he divided his time among the arrivals in the registry room, the detainees held for appearances before the special Boards of Inquiry, and those in the medical wards.

Fiorello La Guardia never ceased to bombard the Washington authorities with suggestions for the improvement of the clearance system and with special intervention in particularly heartbreaking cases where kindness and consideration were particularly needed. The last year of his service was spent as an interpreter for newly arrived immigrants in the Manhattan Night Court. Most of the cases involved minor brushes with the law, and the part-time law school student was able to use some of his newly acquired knowledge. After his graduation he successfully passed his bar examinations and resigned from the Immigration Service in October, 1910.

The interpreter led his manifest group through the main doorway, and directed them up the right stairway to the registry room. The guards at the top and the waiting doctors were usually able to identify the nationality of the majority of the group, and they often made this a game.

The best way to visualize the inspection and clearance procedures in the second floor registry room is to see the floor as viewed from the gallery. Until 1910, when it was partitioned into offices and file rooms, interested visitors could obtain gallery passes to observe the activities below.

To the spectator in the gallery, the huge room in some ways resembled a slaughterhouse, for it consisted of a series of mazes planned to guide the groups of immigrants through the clearance processing.

The area where the medical examinations were given was at the top of the stairs in the eastern half. This was partitioned by iron piping into large open spaces across which the immigrants moved past the teams of doctors. A few screened units held those detained. The rest of the area was divided into small waiting units lined on both sides with wooden benches; after completing the medical inspections the groups waited here until called for the main inspection.

This was conducted in the western half of the room. Twenty-two long aisles were marked off by rows of pipes to a height of 12 feet. These aisles or lanes were paired; in one the immigrants waited on benches until moved along by guards into the adjoining lane, where the interrogation was to be conducted by an immigration officer who was seated at a high desk at the far end. Half the lanes were used by groups from one ship, the other half by those of another.

The prison-like arrangement controlled the large number of groups who were in the various stages of the processing at the same time, and kept individuals from straying from their group.

The room was well-lighted from large side windows extending to the vaulted roof. The air was kept fresh and the floors and benches were immaculately clean.

The average immigrant followed this standard procedure path through the registry room:

1. Medical examination: mental, head and body.
2. Medical examination: eyes.
3. Wait with manifest group in pen.
4. Immigration line inspection, with interpreters; examination on selected manifest questions. If cleared, immigrant given "Admitted" card. If detained, marked appropriately.

What took place in the registry room was of crucial importance to the newcomer.

7

Meeting the Doctors

Those seeking entrance to the United States were faced all along the way through Ellis Island by questioners. The government inspectors were probers for the facts which would enable them to determine whether the door should be opened to those who were knocking. At each stopping point on the second floor of the main building, the registry room, through which every one of the 16 million immigrants passed, the alien was met by an interrogator.

The newcomer had been drilled in answers to make and had been briefed on his behavior. He had been told that two things were important above all others: he must prove to be disease-free, and he must create the impression that he would be able to make his own living (the technical term was "not likely to become a public charge"). The various questions on the manifest could have been answered by deception, hesitation and outright lying. But the medical officers, experts in the detection of disease and deformities, could seldom be fooled.

The United States Public Health Service was given the legal responsibility of excluding from admission to the United States aliens with the following stated medical defects: ". . . all idiots, imbeciles, feeble-minded persons, epileptics, insane persons; persons of constitutional psychopathic inferiority, persons with chronic alcoholism . . . ; persons afflicted with tuberculosis in any form or with a loathsome or contagious disease; persons not comprehended within any of the foregoing excluded classes who are found to be and are certified by the examining surgeon as being mentally or physically defective, such physical defect being of a nature which may affect the ability of such alien to earn a living. . . ."

The all-encompassing medical inspection apparently prescribed and expected under the various laws—the first in 1891, frequently revised, and the later major ones in 1907 and 1917—was impossible from the standpoint of both numbers and time. The inspection was therefore mainly directed toward the detection of the obvious physical defects such as lameness, blindness and deafness; easily recognized mental defects; and special attention to the most serious of the "loathsome" contagious diseases, those of the skin, scalp and eyes.

The doctors performing what was termed the "line" inspection in the registry room were by training and experience almost incredibly adept in detecting almost instantaneously those who should be detained for further examination. The examination was conducted according to a system which was efficient but callous, and the result of many years of development. The major specifications were two: the line should be spaced so that an inspector could have a full view of the alien as he approached, and the line should move forward as rapidly as possible. All decisions were therefore immediate; any doubts resulted in detention.

Those who were to be detained were identified by a chalk mark made on their coats.

Should the alien be suspected of mental defects, an X was marked on his coat at the front of his right shoulder; if some definite symptom had been detected a circled X was used. A plain X lower on the right shoulder indicated that a deformity or disease was suspected.

A few of the more general and most often used of the code symbols will indicate how simply the system operated. B indicated back; C, conjunctivitis; CT, trachoma; E, eyes; F, face; Ft, feet; G, goiter; H, heart; K, hernia; L, lameness; N, neck; P, physical and lungs; Pg, pregnancy; S, senility; and Sc, scalp. Even if an individual was marked early in the examination he continued in the inspection procedure. Only at its termination was he directed to the rooms set aside for further examinations. The coats of many immigrants bore more than one chalk mark.

The policy of caution, which might fittingly be termed "when suspicious, use the piece of chalk," resulted in an over-all 15 per cent being marked for further examination.

Two manifest groups were inspected simultaneously by two teams of examining doctors spaced about thirty feet apart so that the flow would be fairly continuous. The examining area was fairly large because the inspectors needed to see their subjects both from a distance and in action as they walked. Therefore each individual was observed both at rest and in motion.

The rules required that the medical inspection take place in daylight rather than under artificial light. This frequently made it necessary for barge loads arriving late in the day to remain on the Island overnight. Another regulation stated that, whenever possible, baggage should not be carried because of the abnormal conditions of breathing, exertion and posture involved. Most of the immigrants therefore deposited their hand baggage in a waiting-room cubicle and picked it up later.

The first doctor carried out an all-embracing general inspection, looking for both mental and physical defects. As the immigrant approached, the officer gave him a quick glance. Experience enabled him immediately to take in six major details: the scalp, face, neck, hands, gait and general condition, both physical and mental. When the individual halted, the first doctor, with the help of an interpreter, asked one or two questions such as age, destination, future work plans, etc., enough to determine whether he was attentive and alert, an intimation of his mental condition. The chalk was used wherever doubt existed.

The doctors developed special techniques to improve the validity of the medical examination. For instance, if the immigrant was wearing a high collar, the officer opened the collar and unbuttoned the upper shirt button to see whether a tumor or goiter existed. The hand, scalp and eyes were the important area to be particularly watched. A hat was always removed so that the hair and scalp might be observed. All children over two years of age were taken from their mothers' arms and made to walk.

The second examiner of the medical team sought most specifically to identify the contagious diseases termed "loathsome" in the law, that is, those which "excite abhorrence and loathing by reason of the knowledge of their existence."

Favus, a type of ringworm, was the "loathsome" disease

the inspector first looked for; others were leprosy and the venereal diseases. The official definition of favus was "a contagious disease of the skin, especially of the scalp, due to a parisitic fungus, marked by the formation of yellow flattened scabs and baldness." The disease was also frequently found under the fingernails.

The danger of favus was that it was easily transmitted by contact, direct as well as indirect, through hairbrushes, towels, or linen. It was regarded as being practically incurable.

The detection of favus was made more difficult because it could rather easily be concealed. The wearing of a hat or gloves and a well-trained pompadour hair style were always suspicious signs.

The only communicable disease specified by name in the immigration laws was tuberculosis, which was one of the leading causes of death in the United States, particularly in slum tenements. Only a few cases of this urban disease were detected by the inspectors in each shipload of the "new" immigrants, who for the most part came from agricultural communities and small towns.

The doctors sometimes felt it necessary to detain immigrants singly or in groups for two other reasons, lousiness and filthiness. If not discovered and controlled, a lice invasion of the ship's steerage would result in the necessity to delouse all passengers at Ellis Island. Sometimes scores of aliens who might not have bathed or removed their clothes since they had left their homes would be forced to bathe before they were cleared.

Still in single file, the aliens moved on to the end of the long aisle, where they stopped before two more doctors, behind whom were nurses, and tables holding towels and basins filled with disinfectant solutions.

These "eye men," each examining an alternate immigrant, looked for defects of sight which might limit the activities of the newcomers. But most of all their special province was the detection of diseases of the eye which were almost incurable, particularly trachoma, one listed as grounds for exclusion. The examination for the latter was accompanied by acute momentary discomfort and pain. This fact was spread in such vivid terms, out of all proportion to the truth, that a great number of immigrants were terror-stricken when they approached these "men with the towels."

Trachoma is a form of conjunctivitis characterized by granulation under the eyelids that is not visible to the naked eye. A highly communicable disease classified in 1897 as "loathsome and dangerous to public health," trachoma seriously affects the eyesight and could cause blindness. The disease was the source of over half the medical detentions, and exclusion was mandatory on the basis that the person affected might become a public charge.

Only when the doctor snapped back the lids—the medical term is evert, to turn outward or inside out—could it be detected. The instrument used in those days was a glove buttonhook. The resulting pain and soreness was due to the sensitivity of the inner eye.

After the eye examination those bearing chalk marks were taken to various inspection rooms at the western end of the registry room. One parent, usually the mother, always accompanied an underage child, so that some families were separated at this point.

Those who had passed the line medical examination went to one of the small waiting areas marked by their manifest letter, until they were summoned to assemble for the "primary" line inspection.

Only this last step remained before the immigrant gained his long-sought goal.

8

The Final Barrier

By now the immigrants in a manifest group were so accustomed to waiting that they were not at all surprised to be led into the enclosure surrounded by pipe barriers, where they would sit on the wooden benches until called for the final examination, based on the manifest information.

"By this time we had gone through so many experiences since arriving that we were completely exhausted," Russian-born Tania Lipkovka, who had passed through the Island in 1912, recalled. "Yet we all knew the importance of this final inspection. A few in our group had been sent to the Island by the medical men but the rest were ready to get things over. Most of us were going beyond New York City and we just wanted to get on the trains.

"However, most of the warnings we had were about the checking of the lists [manifests]. Someone said that the men were hired to trick us into saying the wrong thing. On the boat people had practiced what they would say, with one person taking the part of the officer. He would ask them questions and when they answered he would ask more, trying to get them mixed up just like lawyers do. However, almost everybody agreed it was better to tell the truth, but some said we should remain silent and pretend not to understand, answering only 'yes' and 'no' and making the officer ask many questions. This was so they would not trick us.

"Quite a few people on the boat had some extra money put aside to pay the American inspectors and the American doctors. This was what they always did at home and they could not understand that they would not have to pay at Ellis Island.

"Even though I knew that my papers were in order and that I would not have to tell any lies, I was very nervous because I felt something might still go wrong for me. This big room had high ceilings and all around there were many groups going through the various lines, and there was a hum of voices which bounced down from the roof. No one was shouting; it was really more quiet than you would suppose with all those people.

"While we waited—almost an hour because there were others before us—we talked of other things to take our minds off the examination. We talked mostly of our futures. We realized that when and if we passed we would all go our separate ways and probably never see each other again. Even so, we exchanged addresses so we could keep in touch."

What they waited for while sitting on the hard benches surrounded by their hand baggage was officially termed the "primary line inspection."

When a group including all the names on a particular manifest were conducted with their hand baggage from the enclosure in which they had been waiting, they took seats on benches along a narrow aisle, moving into an adjoining aisle when a guard called out their manifest numbers. At the end of this second aisle was the primary-line inspector, sitting on a high stool with the manifest on the desk in front of him.

An interpreter, sometimes two, stood next to him and acted as intermediary when necessary.

The immigration inspector was to examine each alien as to his right to enter the United States: the various laws specified that only those immigrants be allowed to land "who have an undoubted right to enter." As an Immigration Commissioner once said, "the legal theory that a person is innocent until he is proved guilty has no place in the procedure at our immigration stations. There the burden rests altogether upon the immigrant to prove, against all arguments, his right to enter."

It was, he continued, an absolute necessity to examine each alien with care, with a view to admitting none except those who were obviously likely to be of use to the communities in which they settled, and rigorously to send back all those who gave evidence of their likelihood of becoming a detriment to the community.

The inspector therefore had a mandate to use his discretion in carrying out the intent of the various laws in fairness and equity, without bias and prejudice. He was expected to detect deceit, trickery and evasion and to watch for aliens attempting to enter with borrowed, transferred or forged papers.

The inspector was required to possess an endless fund of patience, an honest desire to exercise judgment with fairness and an awareness of the implications of his decisions. In his cross examination he recorded changes in or additions to manifest information in a registry book, and filled out the necessary forms.

The immigration officer was not the final arbitrary decision-maker, however. A system of Boards of Special Inquiry, discussed later, guaranteed a hearing on points which the inspector had challenged or felt needed further investigation.

The first question asked, partly as a check on that given in the manifest, was the name. A surprising number of aliens had decided to take a new name in the new life, one simpler than the multisyllabic, almost unpronounceable and unspellable name they bore. Such a change was common when later applying for naturalization (citizenship) papers. But a certain number wanted the new name entered on the official register. For example, scores of immigrants with names ending in "ski" or "sky" simply dropped the last syllable.

Others could not spell their names, and the helpful official suggested a simpler "Americanized" one which was readily accepted.

The uncle of Elia Kazan, the stage and film director, thus changed his name from the Greek Avraam Elia Kazanjoglou to Joe Kazan when he arrived in 1896. Brought to America when he was four, the future director kept his first name Elia—he was named after his uncle—and also became Kazan.

The 1963 motion picture *America America,* which Kazan both wrote and directed, is the story of this uncle and his struggles to get to America.

In the film the young man is named Stavros Topouzoglou. After many trials he finally boards ship for New York, but the husband of the woman who has paid his fare vows to have him excluded on arrival. A longtime friend is also in the steerage in a group of shoeshine boys being brought in by a padrone, or labor broker.

The coughing of this friend, named Hohannes Gardashian, reveals to the quarantine officer that he has tuberculosis, a disease calling for mandatory exclusion, and he will, of course be deported. To give his friend Stavros his place Hohannes jumps overboard the night before landing, leaving his passport behind.

In the primary line inspection at Ellis Island, the names on the manifest are read off by the immigration officer. Stavros answers to the name of his friend, Hohannes Gardashian. The official writes the name "Joe Arness" on a piece of paper and says, "If you want to be an American, the first thing to do is to change your name. Hohannes is all you need here . . . Joe Arness."

Sometimes the official misunderstood the name or spelled it as it was pronounced rather than as it was spelled. There is in New York City's Bronx borough a Turkish family named Solomon. Solomon is, of course, a popular Jewish family name and scores are listed in the Bronx telephone directory. But it is certain that only one is Turkish. The Ellis Island inspector misunderstood the name Suleman, which very easily became—and has remained to this day—Solomon.

The most common story, which was told to the author in good faith five times as being true, is probably a bit of folklore which may or may not have happened. At any rate, a German Jew named Isaac was said to have become confused when the officer started questioning him. To the first question "was ist ihr namen?" he was unable to think quickly and answered "Vergessen" ("I forget"). The offi-

cial wrote down "Ferguson" and added the first name he
supplied, "Isaac." So there is supposed to be an Isaac
Ferguson who was named at Ellis Island.

The immigration inspector continued to probe some of
the specific questions. The "payment of passage" item
(number 14) sought to extract from male immigrants
whether they had come, with fares prepaid, as contract laborers, which had been against the law since 1885. He
could immediately check with the question (number 21)
regarding assistance in coming.

Contract laborers were defined in the law as "persons
who have been induced, assisted, encouraged, or solicited
to migrate to this country by offers or promises of employment . . . to perform labor of any kind, skilled or unskilled." Questions in the manifest brought out information
on some of these conditions.

In actual practice, almost every male immigrant had some
assurance of employment in the United States. This was
his security for the future, promised him in most cases by
a relative or friend who assured him that he could be put to
work, a job was waiting. But very often he had signed with
a labor agent who had advanced him the passage money in
return for an agreement to work for the number of months
necessary for repayment, a situation comparable to the
indenture of servants.

These agents operated throughout Europe, always in
direct violation of the American immigration laws on the
subject, the first of which was passed in 1883. But the
economic advantage to employers of importing European
labor at much less than the market rate of wages was so
great that the risk of detection was a gamble worth taking.

The workers were recruited and supplied on order—300 coal miners, 200 textile weavers, 24 glass blowers, 50 marble workers, 50 railway workers to report to Chicago, 100 tunnel diggers, and the like. These requisitions were from specific employers. Some called for skilled workers, but most were for common labor—digging, excavating, construction and the like, the only requirement for which was physical strength. A large number of these workers were illiterate and eager enough to sign away their futures to reach the land of promise. Certainly they had no idea that contract labor was against the law and for that reason their situation was the more pitiful when they were questioned for exclusion.

The author was fortunate in hearing about such a predicament from oldster Anton Petrak, a Slovak who passed through Ellis Island in 1902 when a young man of 20 who "followed the end of the rainbow—yes, we had them in the Carpathian Mountains in the northeast corner of Hungary, where I lived," he said.

"I was a coal miner there and one day a man came to our village," he recalled, "and talked about how much miners were needed in America, especially in Pennsylvania, and how much money was to be made. Well, some from our village had gone and I had started to save money for the trip. I knew to the penny exactly how much I would need. He said there was a job waiting for me once I got to the town called Windber, Pennsylvania, which had just started because of bituminous coal being discovered there. If I was not married I would live in a company boardinghouse and there were a lot of other Slovaks there, too.

"He did not offer to pay my fare, nor did he write down

his promise. He just told me to look him up when I got there. He gave me his name on a card but at that time I could not read. He did say they would see about giving me back the ticket money after I was working there for awhile.

"When I was at Ellis Island I was afraid of the questions because I did not have any piece of paper telling me I had the job promised and I did not even know his address. Some of the men on the boat called me all kinds of names— stupid, dumb, and all that, and they said I would surely be sent back. But I was young and strong and experienced, and I knew I could get some other mining job if this did not work out.

"Well, it didn't. The inspector asked me to tell the interpreter the story, and the promises, and exactly what I was told, and everything. I got all mixed up because he kept saying such things as 'Didn't you know that was against the law?' 'Why do you know so little about him?' and 'Who are you going to see in the mining town?'

"I said I had the ticket and the card, and how would I know about it otherwise and make my plans. Anyway, I could go there and they needed coal miners, and I was strong. I had a little money which I showed them. I think it was $17, but everything was paid and so that was enough.

"Well, the officer gave me a card and I stayed on the Island for a few days while they tried to find out about this man. I had to tell my story to three men [a Board of Special Inquiry] in a small room with an interpreter, not the same one, to help me out.

"But I was lucky. Some other Slovaks from the coal mines came to meet some of my people and they told the men they would promise to take care of me, so I went with them and it turned out all right."

The primary line inspector's role in this episode was to make sure that young Anton had not been duped, that work did await him, that he had paid his own way even though he felt that he had been promised repayment.

Finally came the question (number 15) which the immigrant knew was very important to his future: "Do you have $30? If less, how much?"

The question was more or less a formality. There never has been a monetary requirement for admission to the United States, and the impression, quite prevalent among Americans and aliens alike, that a certain specified sum of money was necessary was quite baseless. The $30 figure, a reduction from $50 which had proved unrealistic in early federal laws, was stated in the manifest law because its framers felt that this sum would form a nest egg for the immigrant and that he would not need to rely upon the promises of his relatives or friends.

The inspector always asked to see the money, since the sum was to be recorded on his registry sheet. Sometimes he would require the assistance of the interpreter when an alien was hesitant or suspicious. Some individuals would immediately produce the foreign bills or coins in a neat pile to be counted. Others would fumble in their pockets and produce a few bits of paper money and, upon urging, would add more. Some presented sealed envelopes which the inspector would tear open and then count the contents.

The Ellis Island officials were aware that immigrants seldom showed all the money in their possession, only as much as they thought was necessary to secure their admission. One who possessed practically nothing would try to maintain that friends were waiting to give him huge sums, or that he would start on a promised job within a few days. As a matter of fact, the inspector weighed such information against the lack of funds, on the basis that an able-bodied man who indicated that he had a useful occupation, particularly a craft, had no fear of rejection.

The officials also took into consideration the fact that the "new" immigrants tended to settle in national or racial groups in their new country. The later arrivals would therefore be welcomed by their own "people" who would protect and assist them in adjusting to the unfamiliar situation. Financial aid formed a major part of such care, and the inspectors recognized that if relatives or friends could not assume the financial burden of aiding the newcomer, a society or group would invariably undertake the responsibility.

The Dillingham Commission's report (see Chapter 10) in 1911 sought to estimate the average amount of money shown to the inspector in an attempt to set a reliable minimum figure in future legislation. The result (based on figures for the period 1905 to 1907, when the "requirement" was $50) was further divided into "old" and "new" immigrants. The former showed a per capita average of $55.20, the latter $20.99. The total average was $30.14, which became the sum required.

It should be pointed out that many aliens who began the journey with much more than the "suggested" $30 had incurred many unforeseen expenses along the way. There was always someone who for a reasonable sum could make the trip a little easier and more pleasant—obtain special foods, supply more comfortable quarters, aid in avoiding a technical requirement, obtain a needed visa without delay, and the like.

All sorts of emergencies en route might wipe out an alien's resources. Literally thousands who had not purchased prepaid railroad tickets and arrived with insufficient funds for the fare found it necessary to telegraph the friends or family whom they were to join and to wait at Ellis Island until the money arrived.

For the inspector, however, the fact that any amount, no matter how small, was shown was sufficient when other facts were brought out.

The inspector paid no attention to whether or not the money was from the same country as the immigrant, because it would all be converted into United States currency. He had a table of values on his desk and was thus able to add up the amounts.

Some aliens might acquire a bit more money on the trip. Card playing aboard ship, trading of currency for the uniqueness of it, the sale of some possession—all might yield foreign currency. Morris Abramowitz, the author's barber, who emigrated from Bucharest, Rumania, earned $30 during the 13-day trip from Antwerp and showed money from four countries.

A very few brought along much more money—from $500 to $1,000. This might represent the savings of months and even years, and was to be the means of establishing a foothold in the strange and new surroundings. Those with such foresight generally brought the money in the form of bank drafts rather than in cash. Such prudent planners rarely mentioned their affluence to their fellow passengers in steerage. Many immigrants who arrived with substantial funds had traveled in first and second class and were therefore exempted from passing through the Island.

The confusion of the alien was often a barrier to the inspector; even with the assistance of an interpreter the answers to some of the questions remained a bewildering puzzle. At the sixteenth question: "Are you going to join a relative or a friend? What is his name and address?" the immigrants brought forth from bosoms, bags and other hiding places pieces of paper bearing illegible penmanship. In checking on the destination question in the manifest, the inspector often had to unravel the mystery not only for his ledger but also for the railroad ticket agent and the baggage master who must send the immigrant on his way.

Most destinations had been written as they sounded or had been copied from undecipherable penmanship in letters from America. "Pringvilliamas," for example, turned out to be Springfield, Mass.; "Chikaigo" was, of course, Chicago; "Neihork, Nugers" was Newark, New Jersey. "Deas Moyness Yova" was Des Moines, Iowa. By long training the inspectors and interpreters came to be experts in unraveling the names of the cities and towns to which immigrants might be going.

Feri Weiss, who was an inspector for many years, recalled some of the most challenging of these geographical puzzles. That a man wanted to go to Lincoln, Nebraska, when his address slip read in almost unintelligible hieroglyphics "Linkinbra" was not so hard to determine, he said, when the inspector knew that he was a farmer, and when, on the reverse side, a passenger had helped by indicating the pronunciation (incorrectly!) as "No-brass-key."

Another difficult problem Mr. Weiss remembered was "Genevood Szekenevno No. 5508 Pillsburs," which required a bit of inspired clue-hunting to decode as Mr. Gene Wood, No. 5508 Second Avenue, Pittsburgh.

This question regarding relatives and friends was investigated very thoroughly in the cases of women arriving alone. The government was particularly solicitous concerning them. Most were temporarily detained until a checkup was completed.

After the key questions had been covered in the primary line inspection, and if all the answers proved satisfactory, the immigrant was entered in the ledger as "approved for entry," and he was given a landing card labeled "Admitted." This permitted him to make arrangements to leave the Island.

During the questioning, the inspector had indicated those who were to be detained for further questioning by using three codes:

T.D.—Temporarily Detained: those who had insufficient funds to proceed to their destinations and who had to wait until money was sent by relatives or friends; those, particularly women, who had to await the arrival of relatives who were to be responsible for them; and those who had to remain because a member of the family had been sent to the Island's hospital or was being held for further questioning.

S.I.—Special Inquiry: those whose problems could be more fairly solved in a hearing before a Board of Special Inquiry consisting of three government inspectors sitting as a court to consider an immigrant's admission or exclusion.

(The operation of these boards is described in Chapter 9.)

L.P.C.—Likely to Become a Public Charge: those who for physical or other reasons appeared unable to make a living or had no relative or friends who might contribute to their support. They were held for appearances before Boards of Special Inquiry.

These detention types were in addition to those who had been held because of the doctors' chalk marks in the medical examinations and had not yet gone through the primary line inspection.

But the majority were usually approved for entry. For example, during the year 1911, 605,000 of the 637,000 immigrants passing through the Island were promptly admitted on the first inspection.

A new procedure was added to the primary line inspection when the literacy test became an admission requirement in 1917 (see Chapter 11). With a few exceptions, the examination was given to all immigrants over 16. The law required the test to cover the ability "to read matter printed in plainly legible type and in a language or dialect designated by the alien."

The interpreter used printed and numbered test slips of uniform size, with from 30 to 40 words in ordinary use. Test cards were available for 40 languages and dialects.

Before this requirement 21 per cent of all immigrants were illiterate; thereafter, knowing of the test's importance, most arrivals had thoroughly prepared themselves for it. The introduction of the test placed a new burden on the Ellis Island officers, particularly the interpreters, just at the time when the number of postwar immigrants was increasing.

As they left the inspection aisle, the immigrants remaining in the manifest group were divided into three groups: those detained, those going to New York City, and those traveling to destinations beyond.

Those in the first group went to the smaller rooms on the same floor in order to be questioned further. In some cases the interrogation could be completed in a very short time; others would have to remain on the Island.

The fortunate second group, bound for New York City (about 29 per cent of the total number of immigrants), had only to stop at the first floor baggage room to arrange for delivery of their heavy baggage to their addresses in the city.

Now these New York-bound immigrants left the building en route to the ferry which would take them to the terminal at the Battery. The walks were enclosed by wire netting all the way to the boat. On the other side of the netting an expectant crowd of relatives and friends awaited them. The excitement was boundless.

In a babel of tongues they shrieked all sorts of questions across the space, yelling and gesticulating. When the immigrants arrived at the landing, the gates were opened and the reunions were highly emotional. Mothers and sons, sisters and brothers, cousins, friends, sweethearts were reunited, and in these few moments of joy the long years of sorrow and separation were forgotten. Smiles and tears mingled, tears of happiness that the soil of the American mainland was just a mile-long boat ride away.

Still other friends and relatives waited at the Battery ferry terminal, sometimes for hours. When the boat was docked, there were many more tears of joy and warm welcomes in all tongues as the last gates to the New World were thrown open wide.

The third group, those who were going by railroad to localities beyond New York, followed a prescribed route: the money-changing wickets on the second floor, and on the first floor the railroad ticket offices and the baggage room; and, finally, the waiting room, where they would remain until summoned to board a barge which would take them to the appropriate railroad terminal or to the proper connecting point.

Money was exchanged by cashiers at half a dozen wickets located at the western end of the registry room near the stairs. These brokers changed the immigrants' gold and silver coins as well as bank notes and drafts into United States currency at the market rates of exchange plus a small fee. Those arriving with little money converted the full amount, since they would need funds almost immediately. Others with bank drafts usually waited until they were settled so that they need not carry large sums with them. The exchange rates were marked on boards, and the broker was required to pay the current rates and to give the immigrant a written receipt of the transaction.

The money exchange, baggage transfer and lunch counters and restaurant on the Island were operated by concessionaires who had been the highest bidders for the privileges. They operated under government supervision; rules and new bids for the contracts were required annually. As the number of immigrants mounted the sums involved became enormous, not because of any increase in the charges fixed by the officials but because of the volume of customers. If a concession was not operated with full satisfaction, the holder was not permitted by law to bid again. As a result the services functioned efficiently and reliably.

The immigrant now descended the stairs and turned right into the railroad room. In the early days of the Island all the leading railroads sold tickets there, but later this privilege was narrowed down to an immigrant clearing house of the Trunk Line Association, made up of the major railroads running to the west and south. The alien was therefore assured that the most direct route was followed. Rates were standardized and competition was virtually eliminated.

Tickets were either purchased on the spot with the newly acquired United States currency, or, if the immigrant possessed a ticket voucher already obtained as a part of the steamship fare, the coupon was paid for by the appropriate line.

Since those with out-of-town destinations totaled a little more than two-thirds of all who passed through Ellis Island, the ticket office was always a beehive of activity. During peak periods 25 tickets were sold per minute. About half of the transactions were in cash and the other half in orders from the steamship companies. One of the Ellis Island Commissioners reported that a daily intake of $40,000 in cash alone was not uncommon.

Twelve men sold tickets at the windows, and linguists representing immigrant aid societies helped in separating the ticket holders into groups by railroad companies.

Ticket in hand, the immigrant stopped off at the baggage room to check his heavy luggage to his destination via the proper railroad.

Until the First World War, the major railroads scheduled special "immigrant trains" made up entirely of coaches. They stopped only at towns or cities where a passenger, or passengers, was to be dropped off. The paternalistic policy of the government was that immigrants should be kept together in groups and dispatched from Ellis Island by barge or ferry to the various stations only a short time before the trains departed. The experience of Castle Garden indicated that immigrants should be protected along their way. Only a limited number of the "Admitted" newcomers going beyond New York City were met by relatives or friends and released in their custody.

Most of the immigrants were now distributed to compartments marked with the name of the railroad on which they would travel. There they awaited the summons to go aboard a railroad ferry which would carry them and their belongings to the station of the particular road, or, if that station was inland, to a point where they could connect with other conveyances which would carry them there.

Matrons, attendants and representatives of the immigrant aid societies helped those going far distances in purchasing food for the journey. Box lunches were available, the size proportioned to the number in the family and the length of the trip. The average price was about fifty cents a person for food enough for three to four meals. The contents for each meal usually included one or two sandwiches, a piece of sausage or a tin of sardines, a hard-boiled egg and a piece of fruit or pie.

Many families, however, preferred to select their own fare. The signs with the prices were in five languages and the choice was wide, the cost moderate (in 1908):

Rye bread, 2 lbs.	10¢	Boiled ham, 1 lb.	30¢
Rye bread, 1½ lbs.	8¢	Corned beef, 1 lb.	25¢
Wheat bread, 2 lbs.	10¢	Sausage sandwiches	13¢
Wheat bread, 1½ lbs.	5¢	2 for 25¢	
Swedish bread, 2 lbs.	10¢	Ham or corned beef	
Rolls	1¢	sandwiches	7¢
Pies	10¢	Cheese sandwiches	5¢
Bologna sausage, 1 lb.	20¢	Cheese, 1 lb.	20¢

A pint of milk cost five cents; a bottle of soda water, ginger ale, sarsaparilla or beer was seven cents. A major complaint was that beer was the only alcoholic beverage sold; this decision was made by Congress itself, to avoid overindulgence. The southern Europeans wanted wine and could not understand why it was not available.

When long waits were necessary for large groups from the same boat, the steamship companies, responsible for the welfare of their passengers until they left the Island, often ordered sandwiches to be distributed to the hungry immigrants, most of whom had not eaten for several hours.

If the delay was to be extended, the passengers were often taken to the restaurant (mess hall) and given sandwiches and a hot dish, perhaps soup. The immaculate tiled dining hall could accommodate 1,100 at a sitting and mainly served detainees who remained on the Island. The long tables were covered with paper which was changed for each meal.

The food was plain but wholesome and the conditions sanitary; the floor was washed six times daily. The serving was cafeteria style and the cost to the steamship company in 1908 was seventeen cents per meal. The standard charge per three-meal day was $1, higher because these meals included a main dish such as a stew, goulash, sausage, or spaghetti.

In the railroad enclosures the last of the many periods of waiting must have seemed interminable. The immigrant was tired but happy in the knowledge that the rest of his way was planned for him.

Finally the call came. Shepherded by a social worker from one of the aid societies, the group walked to the barge which was to take them to the mainland—to the Barge Office if the stations were in Manhattan, or to Jersey City or Hoboken if the trains departed from New Jersey terminals.

The longest and dreaded part of the journey was over. The immigrant had stepped on the soil of his new country. The new life would soon begin.

9

The Detained and Rejected

In contrast to the immigrants who received the "Admitted" cards were those comparatively few (never more than five per cent) who had been drawn from the mainstream and were required to remain on Ellis Island until questions regarding their acceptance or rejection could be settled.

Four kinds of detentions had been indicated and marked by the officials during the medical and primary line inspections: those held for further medical examination, indicated by the doctors' chalk marks; and the three codes used in the primary line inspection—T.D., temporarily detained; S.I., special inquiry; and L.P.C., likely to become a public charge, which was always considered by the Boards of Special Inquiry.

The first type of detainees, those chalk-marked in the medical line inspection, formed the largest number. This was because three distinct and well-defined classes of "defectives" were described in the laws for the benefit of the medical inspectors. The major diseases and disorders for which exclusion was mandatory under the law have been described in Chapter 7—contagious and "loathsome" diseases and mental handicaps.

Immigrants having identifiable contagious and "loathsome" diseases remained in the special hospital on the southern section of the Island, nearest to the Statue of Liberty, until they could be deported.

These mandatory exclusions were most tragic and often heartbreaking. The discovery of such "loathsome" diseases as favus or trachoma, occurring most often in the young, for example, always led to the enforced separation of family members, since the law required that one parent accompany the afflicted minor child when he was deported. Upon receiving the doctors' certified recommendation of exclusion on mandatory grounds, the Boards of Special Inquiry, without a hearing, approved a legal order for deportation.

Another type of medical detainee was those marked with an X or a circled X to indicate suspicion of a mental disorder. Such individuals were immediately conducted to an examination room and given simple tests by the same medical officers who had marked them in the inspection. The detection of mental defects was always difficult; suspects must be observed closely. The doctors were able to note the behavior of the waiting aliens and spot certain behavior and physical clues which would merit further testing. Such persons were given a yellow "hold" card which meant that they were to be held in the hospital wing for mental cases in order to undergo a more complete examination. Most were eventually deported.

The second type, T.D. (temporarily detained), were always numerous after the arrival of large steamships bringing hundreds of steerage passengers. Most of them had been so designated for their own protection. This was often misunderstood and even resented by the detainee, and it was only when friends arrived or when he received money and directions of where to go that he comprehended the purpose of the detention. Of course, if deception had been involved, there was no question regarding the immigrant's exclusion.

Many of the problems were cleared up satisfactorily within a matter of hours in further questioning by an officer or by a Board of Special Inquiry (whose work is discussed below). Since the Inquiry rooms were opposite the exits from the inspection lanes the officer might send a T.D. there immediately, particularly if he or she was bound for New York.

One of the most common of these problems was the failure of relatives to call for an immigrant who was "manifested" to them (that is, they had been indicated as the person whom he was joining). This was essential for unaccompanied women and children and older people, who would need the protection of someone in the new situation lest they become objects of public charity (an L.P.C. case). Inspectors were adept in questioning to be sure that, for example, a husband was actually expecting and was able to support his wife and children, a sister was assuming the sponsorship of a wide-eyed 17-year-old girl, or that a son or sons were willing to undertake the legal responsibility for their aged parents.

Above all, such persons were forbidden to leave the Island alone. If no one arrived or sent telegrams to claim them, they were held until someone did. Sometimes this insistence upon the letter of the law, proof in person or writing, appeared both needless and heartless, but this was the government's interpretation of its responsibilities.

If a relative or a friend was far away and the immigrant possessed no letter as evidence, the authorities (or a social worker) might telegraph (this was long before the advent of the long-distance telephone) to the alien's destination to check on conditions. Such a case might require several days. Others were immediately solved by locating the person in or around the Island ferry terminal or at the New York waiting room, the walls of which echoed continually with the names being paged.

One of the most frequent reasons for temporary detention was lack of funds on arrival, due either to poor planning or to unexpected expenses along the way. Such immigrants were not permitted to continue their journeys. When an alien did not possess a prepaid ticket and lacked the money to purchase one, he was of necessity held until the next of kin either sent the money or came for him. The authorities insisted that the ticket or tickets be purchased on the Island and that the relative or friend was willing to receive him.

Another large group of T.D.s were the families of which a member had been hospitalized as a result of disease contracted on board ship and discovered by medical officers or reported by a ship's doctor at quarantine. The most common were measles, scarlet fever, pneumonia, sore throat and bronchitis. Measles was by far the most common children's disease. While the sick member was being treated in the main hospital the others in the family remained in the detention quarters, their expenses paid by the steamship company, until the family could leave together.

Most of the arriving single young women avowed their intention of joining a sweetheart or fiancé. One of the most persistent of all immigration problems, especially in the first two decades of the century, was the operation of procurers and panderers. Therefore, the inspectors seldom accepted a girl's word or even letters and telegrams as evidence that she was telling the truth.

The almost inflexible rule was that either the friend must come to Ellis Island in person or that the girl must remain until a social worker at the destination could undertake an investigation and certify the truth. "Uncles" and "brothers" very often turned out to be nothing of the sort. The luring of girls to America through payment of passage and the promise of a comfortable future far removed from the strenuous peasant life was frequently exposed when the stories of the men failed to coincide with those of the girls.

Some single women arrived with the intention of marrying men they had never seen. But many used the prerogative of a woman to change her mind. Marriage brokers and matrimonial agencies were active in Europe because many single immigrant men wanted wives of their own nationalities, who were not often to be found, particularly in the industrial towns where bachelors lived in boardinghouses.

The bridal candidates sent photographs but the prospective groom did not. Records reveal that upon meeting their prospective husbands at Ellis Island literally scores of these brides-to-be asked to be deported! Stories in newspapers told of future brides meeting and falling in love with a fellow passenger en route, then spurning the waiting bridegroom. Deportation was not, however, the consequence of such a change of heart; if a Board of Special Inquiry was satisfied that the new love was able to support her, she was married on the Island.

Hundreds of reunited couples were married in civil or religious ceremonies on arrival, as soon as the wedding was approved by a Board of Special Inquiry. A Catholic priest was almost always available on the spot, and social workers could easily locate a judge or a Protestant clergyman.

The third detention group was composed of those marked S.I. (special inquiry). These detainees ran a great risk of exclusion, but the immigrant was given an opportunity of stating his case before a final judgment was passed.

The nonmedical, nontemporary detention cases were considered by Boards of Special Inquiry, of which four were continuously in operation at Ellis Island. An idea of their importance can be gained by the fact that 60,000 cases of 900,000 immigrants were handled in 1913.

The authority of these boards was specifically stated in the immigration laws: "Every alien who shall not appear to the examining inspector to be clearly and beyond a doubt entitled to land shall be detained for examination in relation thereto by a board of special inquiry."

The three members of a board were immigration officers, and they held private hearings continuously. The alien, not represented by legal counsel but aided by an interpreter when necessary, presented his own case and defense and was questioned by the officers. If necessary, relatives would send needed papers or affidavits; sometimes they would come to the Island to testify. Social workers in distant cities might make personal investigations and report to the board.

The immigrant might appeal an adverse decision of a board through various channels—the Ellis Island Commissioner and the Commissioner-General of Immigration—to the highest Washington authorities. Relatives would often bombard members of Congress, the President himself, the Commissioner of Immigration and the diplomatic representatives of their native country for intervention in the case, frequently with success. This question of interference and reversal of opinions was frustrating to the immigration authorities, who were helpless to oppose it.

The nonmedical bases for exclusion, all mandatory, as enumerated in the immigration laws were "persons likely to become a public charge, persons who have been convicted of or admit having committed a felony or other crime or misdemeanor involving moral turpitude (i.e., criminals), polygamists, anarchists, prostitutes and procurers, and contract laborers." It will be remembered that some of these items were among the manifest questions.

The "likely to become a public charge" category has already been discussed as one of the types of T.D. cases always considered by the Boards of Special Inquiry.

The contract labor category, already considered in Chapter 8, was one of the major types of cases heard by boards. In spite of continuous legislation excluding them, contract laborers continued to pour into the country and constituted a major problem in determining the admission or exclusion of male immigrants.

Action on the exclusion clause of the anti-contract labor

laws was a function of the Boards of Special Inquiry. The alien himself had often been duped and yet the enforcement of the law called for exclusion and deportation. Objections to the rigid enforcement of this clause were both vocal and constant. So specific was the wording, however, that deportation of an immigrant was mandatory if within a year of his arrival it could be proved that he came under contract.

The period of detention while decisions were being made regarding his exclusion and deportation was one of great emotional stress for the alien awaiting the verdict. For some the final adverse decision literally meant life or death, and to escape deportation they chose the latter. In spite of the lack of privacy and the vigilance of guards, suicides were frequent. The toll through the 40 years has never been publicized, but it was informally estimated as at least 3,000.

A small crematorium located near the powerhouse on the extreme northwest corner of the main Island disposed of the bodies of suicides and those of the hundreds who died in the hospitals or halls over the years. This was the only gesture the government could make for these tragic people who had no hope and rarely any next of kin who could trouble about them in a strange land and situation.

The frequent attempts, particularly by young men, to escape by swimming to the nearby New Jersey shore almost always failed because the swimmer could easily be detected and returned by launch. The comparatively few drownings occurred under cover of darkness when the tides were rising.

As many as 3,000 at one time might be detained on the Island, awaiting either hearings or transportation. The number of deportations was never below 1,000 per month and often totaled eight or ten times that number.

In addition to incoming immigrants, Ellis Island was always the examination and detention spot for citizens or immigrant residents not yet naturalized who were subject to deportation to Europe. These reverse-flow individuals always constituted a part of the Island's population. Other deportees were the stowaways (an average of 300 annually) and alien seamen who had deserted from their ships.

During the two war periods, when the usual flow of newcomers was reduced, Ellis Island sheltered unique types of guests. When the United States entered the First World War in 1917, over 2,000 sailors from ships confiscated in American harbors were interned there for the duration. Thousands of so-called "alien enemies, plotters and agitators" were also detained. Their cases were not considered until after the armistice and hundreds were then deported as "undesirables" under the terms of a wartime Espionage Act.

The most unusual of all types of detainees, however, were the alleged foreign revolutionaries and radicals who were sent to Ellis Island from all over the country after the war was ended. This was the astounding "Red scare" of 1919 with its postwar upsurge of radicalism, bomb outrages and labor unrest. A special act in 1918 called for the "exclusion and expulsion of all United States aliens who are members of the anarchistic and similar classes."

Hundreds of labor agitators, supposed "Bolsheviks" and members of the radical Industrial Workers of the World (I.W.W.), called "Wobblies," were arrested in a countrywide operation. In the first six months of 1920, 5,000 deportation arrest warrants were issued, and the 2,500 actually arrested were held on Ellis Island and given hearings. Only a relatively few were allowed to remain in the country on parole; the majority were deported in ships specially chartered by the government.

Even after the immigrant stream had been reduced to a trickle in 1932 and the processing there ceased, the Island continued to receive and care for those who were sent by the immigration inspectors operating on the steamship piers. Many of these were displaced persons, European refugees and war brides.

Ellis Island continued to be a place of detention until it was abandoned.

10

Improving the Welcome

🔖 The migration from Europe to the United States during the four decades from 1890 to 1930 was the largest continuous mass movement in history. The processing of the majority of the 70 per cent of these immigrants who passed through the Port of New York—over 16 million—represented one of the most complicated and challenging tasks ever undertaken by the United States government. Ellis Island was the locale of this welcoming operation.

The task at the Island was obviously one of the most difficult and delicate in all government service. With admission policies requiring ever more specific standards of bodily health, moral worthiness and the ability for self-support, the duties of those who guarded this gateway were of the highest importance. The spirit with which the Island's battalion of inspectors, doctors, guards and matrons approached their work and the thoroughness with which they carried out their duties were of crucial importance. The principal requirement in their performance was a broad human sympathy which insured the incoming alien not only justice but kindliness, not only a stern protection of his rights but a warm-hearted concern for his comfort in a very difficult situation.

The handling of thousands of immigrants daily required haste, and the alien easily lost his identity and became a mere number. During 1907, 5,000 was fixed as the maximum number of immigrants who could be examined in one day, even with the full staff on duty. Yet during the spring of that year (see Chapter 11) more than 10,000 immigrants arrived on many days.

For many years the cries of outrage against the treatment of immigrants and the "exposures" of "deplorable, crowded, pitiful, corrupt, evil, distressing, unhealthy, lamentable" (all these and many more sensational adjectives were used) conditions appeared in newspapers and magazines with great regularity. Isolated incidents were made to appear as routine, the cruelty of decisions was emphasized with no mention of their purposes, and the officials were painted as insensitive machines.

Such stories, often pure fantasies far from the truth, invariably had reader appeal. Henry Pratt Fairchild aptly described the frequent basis of such stories. "Is it surprising," he wrote in 1913, "that the casual and tender-hearted visitor who leans over the balcony railing or strolls through the passages, blissfully ignorant of the laws and of the meaning of the whole procedure, should think that he detects instances of brutality and hard-heartedness? To him the immigrants are a crowd of poor but ambitious foreigners who have left all for the sake of sharing in the glories of American life and are now being ruthlessly and inconsiderately turned back at the very door by a lot of cruel and indifferent officials. He writes to his home paper, telling of the 'Brutality at Ellis Island.' "

The inspectors were generally cast in the role of heartless villains because they were the decision makers. Questions involving the breaking up of families, the wrecking of long-anticipated plans and a host of other human relations presented themselves in a steady stream before an inspector. He was charged with the execution of an ironbound set of laws and regulations into which his personal feelings and inclinations could not be allowed to enter. And so he became the stereotype of the unfeeling public official.

Misconduct and scandal more than once occurred among employees, but they were always fully investigated and punished. In the early 1890s frauds were uncovered in the forging of passports and the acceptance of tips and bribes by inspectors. Several times guards were discharged for maltreatment of immigrants. It was perhaps inevitable that there were times when the guards' patience wore thin with the continual contact with aliens in a state of bewilderment and stupor brought on by the bustle, confusion and size of Ellis Island. As one employee said in his defense, "It is all right to talk of kindness and consideration, but there comes a time, usually of overwork and the pressure of thousands of the waiting, when good intentions are discarded, self-control reaches a breaking point and the immigrants become the victims. Unfortunately they frequently try our patience beyond endurance. The only solution at such times is a vacation, which is exactly what we cannot take during rush periods." And so the pushing, shoving and shouting admittedly occurred and unfortunately were publicized.

As it should be in our democratic system, almost every operating government agency has at one time or another become a target of criticism. Congressional investigations were frequent at Ellis Island. Abuses, delays in the reception of aliens, overcrowding in detention quarters, even the food and baggage concessions, came under fire at one time or another.

Both the House and Senate participated in full-scale investigations through their respective Committees on Immigration, with on-the-spot inspections and abundant testimony in hearings, much of it published in full in official government documents. The major inquiries—in 1903, 1911, 1914, 1916, 1919 and 1923—ended with recommendations regarding needs and improvements. But, as always, improvements required funds for building expansion or personnel increases, and these were seldom forthcoming as a result of the official attention. The improvements in and extension of the Island resulted from budget requests of the Commissioner-General. As will be seen in the next chapter, pleas to Washington for special appropriations or approval of emergency procedures in times of stress too often fell on deaf ears.

Complaints made by immigrants were for the most part made by those of the northwest European countries, particularly the English, Germans and Scandinavians, and resulted from unhappy personal experiences. Complaints very naturally followed when, for example, a Britisher whose financial condition had forced him to travel in steerage was submitted to what one of them called "indignities suffered at being penned up with savage beasts and being treated with no consideration as a human being."

As a matter of fact, the most publicized complaints, with international repercussions, resulted in an official British government protest late in 1922, as a result of accounts of maltreatment presented before both the House of Commons and the House of Lords. English immigrants were said to have been "treated like dogs and fed on bread and water," "citizens were inhumanly kept in cages with people of dirtier and inferior nationalities." The specific incidents cited were multiplied ceaselessly. The influential *Times* of London stated editorially that what most offended the English people was our failure to draw any line at Ellis Island between "immigrants of more or less gentle nature and those whose sensibilities were blunted by poverty."

Finally Sir Auckland Geddes, British ambassador to the United States, visited Ellis Island and made a thorough personal investigation of conditions. What was needed, he maintained, was a new and gigantic building with separate quarters for each nationality! The 1924 Immigration Act, with its increased restrictions, answered the complaints of overcrowding; the influx was never again so great.

Throughout the years the United States Congress was extremely conscientious in considering all the controversial aspects of the immigration problem when framing the continuous flow of legislation. Both House and Senate committees patiently heard testimony on conditions and reforms.

The tremendous surge of immigration in the first decade of the present century took place during the administrations of President Theodore Roosevelt. Some of the growing pains of Ellis Island were made simpler by his cutting of red tape and his insistence upon action. It was Roosevelt who in 1907, following the enactment of a major revised immigration law, ordered "a full inquiry, examination and investigation of the subject," and appointed an Immigration Commission of nine members—three Senators, three Representatives and three Presidential appointees. The purpose was to determine future government policy. For three years experts of the Dillingham Commission (as it was called) conducted studies on every phase of the problem, including the effect of immigration upon the institutions, industries and people of our country. The monumental study, published in 42 volumes in 1911, gave the comprehensive survey intended, and for many years proved to be a mine of information as well as a guide to the framers of later legislation.

The welfare of the individual immigrant was given a great deal of attention by both the government and private organizations. The government's protection of the newcomers from the contract labor agents, sometimes called the *padrone* system, has been discussed. Whenever a new problem needed a solution, the necessary legislation was almost invariably introduced and passed. For example, when minor children (under 16) unaccompanied by parents or guardians began arriving in increasing numbers, a regulation enacted in 1915 required that, regardless of the class of steamship accommodations and the amount of money the minor possessed, he be sent to Ellis Island for investigation and clearance.

We have already considered the attention paid on the Island to unaccompanied women and their protection from panderers. Matrons were always available to care for both married and unmarried women and their children. Women inspectors were tried out in 1903 but discontinued after five months on the basis that as decision makers women were too emotional, and also that matrons were readily available when and as needed.

The most concentrated attention, however, was paid to the problem of improvement in steerage conditions. Representatives of the Dillingham Commission and staff members of both Congressional Committees on Immigration traveled in the guise of immigrants in order to observe conditions firsthand (this was always a favorite practice of journalists) and to report upon them. The resulting legislation outlined requirements of air space, deck space, light, ventilation, food and public rooms. Though such laws were well-intentioned, enforcement was difficult if not impossible because almost all of the immigrant-carrying ships were of foreign ownership and registry.

The greatest contributions to the immigrants' welfare were those of the so-called immigrant aid societies, both private and church-sponsored. Most of their activities were in city slum areas: the neighborhood settlement houses aided the newcomers in the problems of adjustment to American life. The development of the profession of social work was immeasurably furthered by the experiences with the foreign-born.

Many of these societies in the New York area worked continuously at Ellis Island with the enthusiastic approval of the federal Immigration Bureau. No personal problem was too small for the attention of these dedicated workers, and the aid given was indispensable in making the confused immigrant feel both welcome and secure.

Some of the societies worked with a single nationality or race; others, with the aid of interpreters, attempted to serve all. Particularly valuable were the activities of these societies in assisting unaccompanied girls and women and in obtaining information through the investigations of similar agencies in cities throughout the country. Detainees received special attention. Those hospitalized were cheered by the ministrations of such representatives. The activities of these societies have been called the "heart" of Ellis Island.

11

Stemming the Flood

From 1907 to the beginning of World War I the maximum daily quota of Ellis Island remained at 5,000; this had been established as the number of immigrants who could be received and passed if absolutely necessary.

Whenever new or revised immigration laws were being discussed in the United States Congress, rumors of their proposed limitations designed to reduce the flow would bring increased floods of immigrants seeking to arrive before the new laws were enacted.

At such times the arrival of overwhelming numbers of newcomers caused crises at the Island. In the face of bitter complaints and criticisms at each extended though unavoidable delay in handling the continuing tide, immigration officers were forced to make adjustments and abridgements in the ordinary processing steps, and to ask higher officials in Washington for temporary dispensations in carrying out the letter of the law. Exceptions were often authorized on the basis of expediency.

The main adjustment made by Island officials when seemingly endless numbers of steerage passengers waited to be passed was sacrifice of the detailed medical examination. Thousands moved hurriedly past the medical inspectors; only those aliens with the most obvious physical diseases or defects were detained.

Because steamship companies failed to work out cooperative arrival schedules, Ellis Island, even with the 5,000 upper limit, was often pushed beyond its operational capacity. New York arrivals in 1906 and 1907 were particularly numerous (880,000 and over a million respectively) because of a depression in Europe and the enactment of a completely revised immigration law effective in mid-1907. The rush was precipitated by steamship agents in Europe, who spread word that the bases for exclusion were to be considerably expanded (which they were).

On March 30, 1906, more than 11,000 passed through the Island and thereafter the average daily figure was 6,000 until April 17, when the number was 11,745. Records were continually broken, daily quotas were discarded and the inspection was reduced to a rapid passage through the inspection aisles.

To the annoyance of the steamship companies as many as 8,000 to 10,000 aliens were frequently forced to remain on board ships for 24 hours or more until they could be accommodated on the Island. The facilities there were not designed to care for such large numbers.

Sunday and holiday operations were frequent. Yet even these were suspended when the seven-day week proved too much for the overworked employees, whether doctors, interpreters, inspectors, clerks, guards or matrons. But this peak period passed and the normal flow recommenced.

When World War I broke out in Europe the influx was naturally reduced to an all-time low. During our country's involvement in the war as few as 25,000 arrived each year.

The 1917 act, which repealed all previous laws, added the literacy test as a qualification for admission. Any immigrant who was unable to read 40 words in any language was to be excluded. This major barrier was particularly directed against southern and central Europe, where the illiteracy rate ran as high as 50 to 70 per cent.

The first literacy test act (see Chapter 8) had been introduced and passed by both houses of Congress in 1896, only to be vetoed by President Grover Cleveland. Renewed attempts to enact literacy bills in 1898, 1902 and 1906 were all defeated in Congress, and although the measure obtained Congressional majorities in 1913 and 1915, it was vetoed in both cases, first by President Taft and then by President Wilson. A second veto by President Wilson was overriden.

When the gates were reopened after the armistice the rush seemed endless. The beginnings of discussion regarding restrictive legislation and, finally, the introduction of national quotas triggered steamship races bringing unparalleled hordes of steerage passengers who could not legally be turned away.

But as an aftermath of the war, prejudice toward Europeans had flourished. The forces favoring restriction, spearheaded by the Immigration Restriction League, began renewed agitation for stringent reductions aimed specifically against the eastern and southern Europeans. The resulting controversy was both bitter and biased.

The "new" immigrant, formerly welcomed by industry, was "a poison in the blood of the nation," and was therefore to be excluded. The bigotry revealed by the proponents of restriction at that time is almost unparalleled in the history of our country. The only comparative prejudice was toward the Chinese and Japanese, against whom exclusion acts had been passed regularly since 1882, and the Mexicans.

While these acrimonious and heated debates were taking place and the much-discussed quota system, which would reduce the numbers admitted, appeared to be in favor, an economic panic in postwar Europe resulted in a rush to escape from the heritage of desolation left by the war.

When immigration was resumed early in 1920 more than 5,000 aliens in scores of ships of every size poured into New York Harbor every day for 100 consecutive days during February through May. In August the steamship companies announced that all accommodations in steerage were fully booked a year in advance.

The number of arrivals continued to multiply so alarmingly beyond the ability of the officials to pass them through even routinely that the situation became unmanageable. By the last week of September, 1920, all immigration was halted until the congestion was relieved. Near riots and disorders took place in the steerage of docked vessels and even on the overcrowded Island itself. The landing of aliens was stopped for 48 hours while Frederick A. Wallis, Immigration Commissioner for the Port of New York, sought relief from Washington officials, requesting both temporary facilities and the suspension of the ordinary inspection requirements until the accumulated human backlog could be disposed of.

The Commissioner's urgent entreaties were rebuffed; the law was the law, particularly since the pros and cons of immigration restriction were being hotly argued throughout the country. The proponents of the quota system used this "unwelcome, overflowing, and uncontrolled flood of the ignorant and unwashed" (certainly an extreme and insubstantiated generalization) to bolster their arguments.

Congress was in the middle of the battle. The House of Representatives, following the familiar legislative practice of procrastination, authorized its Committee on Immigration and Naturalization on October 31, four weeks after the desperate crisis in New York, to "study the situation." Six weeks later its recommendations were for "new buildings and an increased staff," though these were not backed by any discussions of appropriations!

Somehow both the quarantine and the Island inspectors managed to process the flow with routines cut to the minimum. When the House Committee began hearings on the proposed law in December, 1920, some observers felt that all aliens should be barred for six months, but this suggestion as a solution was obviously unrealistic because of the backlog of visas and ship reservations already issued. The flood continued unabated.

Increasing numbers of ships piled up at quarantine, with ever-mounting costs to the companies and serious disruptions of the sailing schedules. Liners were ordered to their piers to await word of acceptance from Ellis Island. The steerage passengers were held on board because the Public Health Service refused to examine them anywhere but on the Island, which was badly overcrowded with over 2,000 aliens temporarily detained.

On December 29, 1920, 1,050 steerage passengers on the *Olympic*, who had been virtual prisoners for six days at a daily cost to the line of $1,200, were examined and inspected on the pier by special permission from Washington, to permit its long overdue sailing. This was to become a standard stopgap procedure for the next half year until the new law, the Quota Act of May 19, 1921, was passed, to become effective 15 days later on June 4.

This law was a provisional one, admittedly a makeshift to stop the influx until more acceptable legislation could be drafted. The annual quota formula was established as three per cent of each nationality resident in the United States as determined by the census of 1910, with the added provision that not more than 20 per cent of any quota might be admitted in any one month.

The deliberate purpose was rigorously to reduce the numbers of the "new" immigrants while encouraging the continuance of the "old." The totals in the 1910 census reflected the succession of generations of the older established immigrants. Therefore the restrictive quotas, as intended, almost closed the doors to some nationalities in comparison with previous figures.

The annual quota for Italy, for example, was set at 42,057, over a 96 per cent reduction of the Italian immigration from 1911-1920 (1,100,000) and 98 per cent of 1901-1910 (2 million). Since the "old" immigration had substantially decreased during the two decades before this legislation, the 1921 quotas authorized, in fact encouraged, a renewal of "old" immigration.

The immediate effect on Ellis Island was a nightmare, as overloaded ships raced to and from European ports in order to arrive in advance of both the monthly and the ceiling quotas. This was called "breasting the quota tape."

The first year of this quota system (June, 1921 through

May, 1922) brought unprecedented numbers monthly. Some annual quotas were exhausted within two or three months, many within six months. These quotas were fixed in accordance with the government's fiscal year of July 1 to June 30.

The steamship lines did little to reduce the number of steerage passengers or to space their sailing schedules. As a temporary measure all excess quota arrivals were permitted to pass through Ellis Island under bond. The races to arrive before the monthly quotas were exhausted continued for two years.

When discussions of a new quota act began early in the summer of 1923 and the new annual quota allotment began on July 1, a renewed rush forced a final settlement of the involved and continuing problem of Ellis Island overcrowding. When the August quotas of 13 European countries were exhausted within a week, Ellis Island closed for a day. This practice was continued as a means of punishing the steamship companies, which were continuing the races to "dump their human cargoes on Ellis Island as if these innocents were crates or baggage."

The serious crackdown began on August 30 with the surprise drastic ruling that excess-quota immigrants on ships reaching quarantine after 8:30 P.M., the time the port closed, and before midnight, would not be accepted during the month of September. Many companies would therefore be required to transport such steerage passengers back to the European port of origin.

Ships with 9,000 passengers were racing to arrive between 8 P.M. and midnight of August 31, 1923, which would give them precedence in the September quota processing on the next day. Four ships arrived before midnight; the companies were immediately fined $200 for each immigrant on board, though the aliens were eventually admitted to the Island.

Finally the companies agreed under pressure to set up and adhere to regular schedules so that the monthly scrambles might be averted. The congestion ceased when the companies realized that under the strict enforcement of the new quota law the days of the steerage-loaded ships were over.

The 1924 Act, known as the "national origins" Act, again caused crowding at Ellis Island. On June 29, the day before the law became effective, 23 ships were approaching New York with 15,000 passengers.

The terms of this law provided that the quota of any nationality should be "two per cent of the number of foreign-born individuals of such nationality resident in the United States as determined by the census of 1890." By further limiting the annual total of admissions to 150,000, the numbers favored the countries of the "old" immigration of pre-Ellis Island days. Because the "new" immigration was only beginning in 1890, these nationalities were the hardest hit. Italy's annual quota, already ridiculously small, became a minuscule 3,845!

The restrictions of the 1924 Act dealt the death blow both to the traditional crowded steerage and to the importance of Ellis Island. While 315,000 passed through in 1924, the figure was reduced by the new law to 137,000 the next year.

The door was almost completely shut to eastern and southern Europeans. The quotas were non-transferable and

some of the countries of the "old" immigration failed even to approach their allotments. By 1932 only 21,500 immigrants arrived and Ellis Island no longer operated as an immigration reception center.

Beginning in 1943, the Island was used as a wartime detention center for naturalized citizens and aliens until their postwar hearings and possible deportations. Many of these interned individuals, particularly Germans, were not released for six or seven years.

Even this function ceased and in 1954 the station was closed. The last detained alien, a Norwegian seaman who had overstayed his leave, was granted a parole and left the Island by ferry at 10:30 A.M. on Friday, November 12, 1954.

Ellis Island became an abandoned relic of a significantly active period of operation. The deserted buildings and halls, once humming with activity and the babel of many tongues, were now silent. The shrubs and lawns became choked with undergrowth and weeds, and the heavy silence was only occasionally broken by the footsteps of watchmen and police dogs on their lonely rounds.

12

From Ghost Island to National Monument

▶ Now the whole Island stood quiet and abandoned in the busiest harbor in the world, alive only in the memories of the millions to whom it had a very personal meaning.

The government tried to maintain the premises for a few years after 1954. But the cost was too high for a white elephant of a place where no one was living. So the heat, water and electricity were turned off and the only sign of life was the federal guard staff.

A year after its abandonment, in 1955, the Island was declared surplus government property and turned over to the General Services Administration for sale. In such cases local governments are given priority in submitting applications for local use. Both New York State and New York City had considered the location of activities on Ellis Island, but the cost of maintaining such a complex was deemed too prohibitive.

When the "For Sale" sign was put up, the value was set at $6,326,000, the amount the government had invested in it. The price tag, not publicly announced, was said to have been a million dollars, later reduced to $800,000.

However, the use to which the property was to be put by the bidder was one of the major elements to be considered, and the General Services Administration reserved the right to reject any and all private bids. Thus began a series of attempts to sell the property.

Meanwhile, some of those who bitterly protested the idea of putting such a symbol as Ellis Island, with all it represented, on the market began to insist that any private development should be opposed. Soon after the 1956 sale offer, Representatives Emmanuel Celler of New York and T. James Tumulty of New Jersey proposed that it be set aside as a national shrine. "To sell the Island," they told President Dwight Eisenhower, "would be cheap and tawdry." Their protests went unheeded, at that time. Each sale was announced in newspapers (see sample ad on next page).

The 21 bids received in response to the first announcement, when opened in February, 1958, ranged from five cents to $201,000. The nickel bid was from a Philadelphian who wrote: "I would use the Island to build a mansion for myself to live, as I like water and like to watch ships passing by." A 12-year-old New Jersey lad sent a $2 deposit on his bid of $20 so that the Island could be used as an orphanage for foreign children. An association to fight narcotics addiction made a bid of $24.12 in the form of trinkets, baubles and cloth to represent the alleged original purchase price of Manhattan Island from the Indians—an attempt to dramatize their plea that Ellis Island be used as a narcotics research and treatment center. The highest bid of $201,000 was from a builder who planned a commercial development which would include a 600-room hotel, a

GENERAL SERVICES ADMINISTRATION

IS PRIVILEGED TO ANNOUNCE

THAT IT IS NOW AUTHORIZED TO OFFER

ONE OF THE MOST FAMOUS LANDMARKS IN THE WORLD

ELLIS ISLAND

FOR PRIVATE COMMERCIAL USE

SEALED BID SALE

Government Owned Island and Improvements,
New York Harbor, N.Y.

Perfect location and facilities for Oil Storage
Depot, Import and Export Processing, Ware-
housing, Manufacturing, Private Institutions, etc.

The property offered for sale is known as "ELLIS ISLAND" and
is located in upper New York Harbor, approximately one mile
from the southerly tip of Manhattan Island and approximately
one-fifth of a mile from New Jersey. The land area consists of approximately 27.5 acres and is improved with 35 buildings, containing approximately 513,000 sq. ft., divided into the following
categories: 14 office buildings, 11 storage buildings and 10 others
consisting of Greenhouse, Laundry, Power House, Incinerators,
Canteen, Library, Infirmary, Cafeteria, Kitchen, Dining Room,
Post Office, Day Room, Dormitories, Baggage Room and School.
Other improvements on the island consist of wharves and docks,
6435 lin. ft. of masonry seawalls, water system 2 miles of main and
2-250,000 gal. overhead tanks, 640 lin. ft. sewage system, incinerators—three units, fuel oil storage 1-130,000 gal. tank, 1-75,000 gal.
tank, electric distribution 6,000 lin. ft. of main feeders, 88,000
sq. ft. cement sidewalks, 7,000 lin. ft. chain link fence (10 ft.
high). Also included in the offering is the ferryboat "Ellis Island"
which was used for transportation between Manhattan and the
Island, miscellaneous items of machinery and equipment, furniture
and cafeteria equipment.

Museum of New Americans, a language school, music center, swimming pool, marina, heliport and seaplane base. None were accepted.

When 23 new bids were received in the spring of 1959 none were "reasonable in the light of the government's investment and because of its inherent value." The highest offer was $671,000, triple the top bid of the previous year and made by the same builder.

The final bidding in 1960 resulted in 11 offers, all of which were rejected. The highest, the third submitted by the developer, was for $1,025,000. The General Services Administration authorities stated that price was most important in considering commercial offers; "for noncommercial uses price is less of a factor, but backing is important. The Government could sell it for half its fair value for use as a park, or it could give it away for use as a hospital or a school, provided that the appropriate Federal agencies endorsed the proposal."

No further public efforts were made to sell the Island, but in 1962 a New York firm bid $2,100,000 for the property to build a city with apartments for 7,500 permanent residents and a hotel for 500 transients, a yacht basin, shops and supermarkets, banks, restaurants, and the like. Moving sidewalks would make it unnecessary for anyone to use automobiles. Before his death in 1959, Frank Lloyd Wright, one of America's greatest architects, had prepared preliminary sketches. But the plan and bid, even with an accompanying $100,000 letter of credit, were rejected from the standpoint of expressing the meaning of Ellis Island.

Beginning in 1956, the Department of Health, Education and Welfare considered suggestions for the Island's use for health or educational purposes. Many applications were received and plans discussed at length, but none seemed to fit the basic requirement that it be used in "the national interest," and the Department's participation in the disposal ceased in 1961.

Between 1955 and 1962 scores of proposals for utilization of the Island were put forth from time to time by public and private individuals. Some were submitted to the Department of Health, Education and Welfare, but most were doomed to remain in the underdeveloped "dream" stage. Most were noncommercial and would require support from federal, state or municipal funds or aid from private foundations. Almost all of the suggestions had worthy purposes. Only one—for a national lottery center, with legalized gambling—was genuinely controversial. Great care and thought had gone into some of the plans. The variety of suggested uses are evident from this abbreviated list.

Education

1. A private, tuition-free liberal arts college, with an enrollment of 1,000, to be supported by foundations.
2. An advanced school for international education and world affairs.
3. An international university for foreign students.
4. A residential college with an experimental curriculum.
5. A school for juvenile delinquents and dropouts from the New York City system.

Health and Social

1. Treatment center for the rehabilitation of narcotics addicts, using the hospital buildings.
2. Mental retardation diagnostic and training center.
3. Veterans convalescent home and rest camp.
4. Recreational area for the promotion of physical fitness.
5. Outdoor-indoor teenage recreation center.
6. Boys Town.
7. Haven for refugees who have been victims of persecution.
8. Housing complex for old people, including a school of geriatrics.
9. A women's prison.

Miscellaneous

1. Center for international trade, with a permanent world trade fair.
2. Maritime center and nautical high school.

Aside from the ever-present questions of financing and administrative control, the principal objection to most of these proposals was that such uses failed to recognize the Island's past history and importance. Ellis Island was certainly more than a piece of real estate.

During the decade of discussion regarding the sale of the Island or its use for some government-approved purpose, the old question of ownership claims was reactivated. The original decision that it lay within the boundaries of New York State was made in 1834, when only the original three-acre island existed. When the Island was abandoned and offered for sale, New Jersey officials claimed that the two extensions of 24 acres would come under that state's jurisdiction because they were nearer to Jersey City than to New York City. A party of city and state officials, including Mayor Bernard Berry and State Senator James F. Murray, Jr., from Hudson County, inspected the Island with a view to planting the state flag on it to substantiate their claim. The New Jersey State Senate even approved a resolution asking the United States to give it to the state. However, the question of ownership became academic when the government decided to retain the Island as a national memorial to America's immigrants.

While these possible uses were being considered, the idea of a national landmark or historical site continued to gain support. All those who advocated such a plan agreed that Ellis Island, like Plymouth Rock, is an important part of our national heritage.

Castle Garden, the first immigration depot in the United States and the predecessor of Ellis Island for the Port of New York, had already been preserved as a harbor fort, as Castle Clinton National Monument. The Ellis Island Immigrant Station remained the most important, if not the only, such station left standing.

A study by the National Park Service conducted during 1963-1964 outlined the reasons why Ellis Island should become a national monument under its jurisdiction. The Subcommittee on Intergovernmental Relations of the Senate Committee on Government Operations, which was holding hearings, recognized the Island's importance as a reminder of a part of our American heritage and history.

The Subcommittee accepted the recommendations of the National Park Service report in mid-1964, and Secretary of the Interior Stewart L. Udall publicly proposed Ellis Island's addition to the Statue of Liberty National Monument and its development in conjunction with a future Liberty State Park, proposed for the nearby Jersey City waterfront. The Statue of Liberty had been declared a National Monument in 1924, and in 1956 the name of Bedloe's Island, its site, was changed to Liberty Island.

Hearings had been held earlier in a House Subcommittee to frame an appropriation bill for the remodeling and rehabilitation work, and the sum of $6,000,000 had been appropriated for the project.

At the same time that President Lyndon Johnson officially proclaimed Ellis Island a part of the Statue of Liberty National Monument, on May 11, 1965, Congress was considering a completely revised immigration bill which was intended to correct the inequities of existing laws. The President therefore used this occasion to remark, "I hope that this Congress will draw on the lessons of Ellis Island and enact legislation to provide America with a wise immigration policy adapted to the needs of the 1960s."

The new bill was passed on October 3, 1965, and the Chief Executive appropriately signed it on Liberty Island, in the shadow of the Statue of Liberty, at a desk facing Ellis Island. The law abolished the 41-year-old national-origins quota system established in 1924, which had marked the beginning of the Island's decline as a reception station. The new law emphasized as a criterion for admittance the skills possessed by the prospective immigrant rather than his native country.

Architect Philip Johnson, who is well-known for the designing of many modern buildings including museums in Fort Worth, Texas, and Utica, New York, as well as the new wing of the Museum of Modern Art in New York City, was immediately awarded a contract to prepare plans for the development of the Island. His proposals "to stabilize the ruins" were announced on February 25, 1966.

Two of the largest buildings are to be preserved—the main reception building and the hospital unit on the first extension, Island Number 2. These buildings will be cleared of all glass and wood, and trees and vines will be planted outside and encouraged to grow over and through the stone walls, turning them into vine-covered ruins. Pedestrian walkways will wind through the gutted buildings. "The point, of course," said architect Johnson, "is to keep the nostalgia and let the spectator himself re-create the feelings of those hard times." This type of ruins-memorial has been widely used in Europe, where war-damaged churches and buildings have been left standing amid the modern reconstruction.

In contrast to the old buildings, a modern structure that the architect calls "The Wall of the 16 Million" will rise 130 feet above the harbor on the side nearest the Statue of Liberty. "A truncated, hollow cone three hundred feet in diameter at the base," the descriptive plan reads, "the concrete structure will be ringed inside and out by spiral ramps eight feet wide leading to and from viewing points at the top. A pool one hundred feet in diameter, surrounded by statuary, is planned for the center of the structure.

"Between the vertical ribs of prestressed concrete that will line the outside of the building the architect hopes to place plaques listing the names of as many as possible of those who passed through the station between 1892 and 1954. The names will be taken from ships' manifests of those years and will be photoengraved on metal. Visitors searching for their own names or those of relatives or friends will be able to find them by 'looking hard.' "

Toward the New Jersey side of the Island the plan includes a picnic ground. On the north shore will be a fortress-shaped restaurant with slots for windows, so that every diner will have a view of the harbor and the Manhattan skyline.

The Island will thus combine the features of a shrine, a park and a tourist attraction.

On the New Jersey shore nearby, the plan calls for the creation of a 400-acre Liberty State Park, as a gateway to Ellis Island, which will be connected with it by a causeway. The park will eventually contain recreation facilities, including tennis courts, playing fields, a concert hall, a marine museum and a 20-story tower topped by several floors of restaurants and sightseeing areas. Thus the purely recreational aspects of the plan will not be located on Ellis Island itself.

The third link in this chain is, of course, the Statue of Liberty National Monument, 1,700 feet to the southeast of Ellis Island. A Museum of Immigration is to be located in its pedestal.

So Ellis Island is to live again, as a memorial to those who passed through this Golden Door.

When a contemporary American visits the completed national monument and locates the name and manifest information of one or more of his immigrant ancestors, he will feel a glow of pride in the knowledge that they were a living part, however anonymous, of a unique phase of American history.

Others will realize, perhaps for the first time, the Island's significance as the gateway to the United States for the millions of aliens who became citizens and were absorbed into the life of our country, truly a nation of immigrants.

Chronology of Immigration
and Ellis Island

1855 Castle Garden immigrant depot begins operation for Port of New York.

1882 First general federal immigration law enacted August 3. State boards, under contract to the Secretary of the Treasury, to inspect immigrants. Financed by head tax of fifty cents.

1883 Federal contract with state of New York to continue operation of Castle Garden.

1885 First federal law prohibiting importation of contract laborers (amended in 1887 and 1891).

1886 Statue of Liberty dedicated.

1890 Castle Garden closed. Immigration inspection operates (as of April 19) under federal government at Barge Office in Battery Park while Ellis Island is prepared.

1891 Immigration placed wholly under federal supervision. Superintendent of Immigration appointed under Treasury Department.

1892 Ellis Island opens as Immigration Station on January first.

1897 Disastrous fire on June 14. Activities transferred to Barge Office until December, 1900.

1900 Island Number 2 added with hospital building.

1900   New fireproof buildings at Ellis Island occupied on December 15.

1906   Largest number of daily arrivals (11,745) at Ellis Island in its entire history—April 17.

1907-1910 U. S. Immigration Commission under chairmanship of Senator William Dillingham, provided by law of 1907, studies all aspects of immigration. Final report (42 volumes) published in 1911.

1907   Peak year of immigration from Europe. Largest number of annual arrivals (1,123,842) at Ellis Island in its entire history. Highest numbers of Austro-Hungarians, Greeks and Italians passed through.

1913-1914 Prewar crest of European immigration.

1913   Island Number 3 added with isolation hospital for contagious diseases.

1916   Black Tom explosion on July 30 almost blows Ellis Island out of existence.

1917-1919 Ellis Island used as a hospital.

1917   Literacy test for immigrants adopted after four Congressional defeats and four Presidential vetoes.

1919   Red scare results in detention of anarchists on Ellis Island.

1920-1921 Postwar immigration rush prior to enactment of 1921 restrictive law.

1921   First Quota Act (provisional) enacted on May 19. Three per cent of each nationality in 1910 census to be admitted annually. Results in immediate decrease in southern and eastern European immigrants.

1924   "National Origin" Act, effective July 1, sets annual quota of each nationality as two per cent of such foreign-born in 1890 census. Ceiling set at 150,000. Becomes fully operative in 1929.

1925   Inspection by American consular officers begins at European ports of embarkation.

1932   Immigrant processing at Ellis Island ceases. Island becomes a detention and deportation station.

1943-1949 Ellis Island used as wartime detention center.

1954 Ellis Island closed on November 12.

1956 Island declared surplus property by General Services Administration. Offered for sale.

1958 Bids on first sale opened on February 14. Three subsequent sales, the last in 1960.

1965 Ellis Island declared by Presidential Proclamation on May 11 to be a part of the Statue of Liberty National Monument.

1965 New, liberalized immigration bill, passed on October 3, abolishes national origins quota system as of June 30, 1968, meanwhile pooling quota numbers.

1966 Design plan for Ellis Island, including Wall of the 16 Million, unveiled by Secretary of the Interior Stewart L. Udall on February 24.

Sources and Readings

Only one full-length book has been written on Ellis Island, *In the Shadow of Liberty,* by Edward Corsi, who was U.S. Commissioner of Immigration and Naturalization, New York District, from 1931 to 1934. For specific information on the Island's internal operations, the author has relied mainly on contemporary articles in New York City newspapers, particularly the *Times* and *Daily Tribune,* as well as periodical articles. The list below is intended to guide the reader to sources which are not too difficult to locate.

Immigration—General Works
(Special treatments of restrictive legislation are listed under Chapter 11)

Abbott, Edith, ed. *Historical Aspects of the Immigration Problem: Selected Documents.* Chicago, University of Chicago Press, 1926.

Abbott, Edith, ed. *Immigration: Select Documents and Case Records.* Chicago, University of Chicago Press, 1924.

Fairchild, Henry P. *Immigration: A World Movement and Its American Significance.* N.Y., Macmillan, 1933.

Handlin, Oscar, ed. *Immigration as a Factor in American History.* Englewood Cliffs, N.J., Prentice-Hall, 1959. Paperback, Spectrum, S-2.

Hansen, Marcus L. *The Immigrant in American History.* Cambridge, Harvard University Press, 1940. Paperback, Harper Torchbooks, TB 1120.

Jones, Maldwyn A. *American Immigration.* Chicago, University of Chicago Press, 1960. Paperback, Chicago History of American Civilization Series, CHAC-11.

Kennedy, John F. *A Nation of Immigrants.* N.Y., Harper & Row, 1964. Paperback, Rev. and enl. ed., Popular Library, PC 1044.

U.S. Immigration Commission (Dillingham Commission), 1907-1910. Reports. Washington, Government Printing Office, 1911. 42 v. Abstracts are given in volumes 1 and 2. Published also as Senate Documents, 61st Congress. A summary of the findings is Jenks, Jeremiah, and Lauck, W. Jett, eds., *The Immigration Problem.* 6th ed. rev. & enl. N.Y., Funk, 1926. An analysis is found in Handlin, *Race and Nationality* (see entry under Chapter 11).

The 1965 Revised Immigration Law
American Academy of Political and Social Science Annals, number 367 (September 1966) is devoted entirely to the law.
"Historic Homage." *Time,* Vol. 86 (October 1, 1965), pp. 27-28.

Chapter 1—The Gateway

Ellis Island—General

Corsi, Edward. *In the Shadow of Liberty: The Chronicle of Ellis Island.* N.Y., Macmillan, 1935.

Foster, Milton H. "A General Hospital for All Nations." *Survey,* Vol. 33 (February 27, 1915), pp. 588-590.

"Growth of Ellis Island." *Scientific American,* Vol. 120 (April 26, 1919), pp. 427, 442 and cover.

Harrington, John W. "New Clearing House for Immigrants." *Harper's Weekly,* Vol. 45 (January 19, 1901), p. 73.

Chapter 2—Emigration from Europe

Handlin, Oscar. *The Uprooted.* Boston, Little, Brown, 1951. Paperback, Grosset's Universal Library, UL-23. pp. 7-36.

Shaler, Nathaniel S. "European Peasants as Immigrants." *Atlantic Monthly,* Vol. 71 (May 1893), pp. 646-655.

U.S. Immigration Commission. *Emigration Conditions in Europe.* Reports, Vol. 4 (also 61st Congress, 2d Session, Senate Document 748).

Chapter 3—Leaving the Old World

Abbott, Edith, ed. *Immigration*. Chicago, University of Chicago Press, 1924. pp. 72-79.

Fairchild, Henry P. *Immigration*. N.Y., Macmillan, 1933. pp. 171-176.

Sherwood, Herbert F. "Silent Keeper of the Gate: Medical Examination of Immigrants." *Outlook*, Vol. 89 (June 6, 1908), pp. 289-296.

Chapter 4—Voyage to the Future

Abbott, Edith, ed. *Immigration*. Chicago, University of Chicago Press, 1924. pp. 82-93.

Brandenburg, Broughton. *Imported Americans*. N.Y., Stokes, 1904. pp. 171-197. Same in *Leslie's Monthly Magazine*, Vol. 58 (May 1904), pp. 69-78.

Durland, Kellogg. "Steerage Imposition." *Independent*, Vol. 61 (August 30, 1906), pp. 499-504.

Fairchild, Henry P. *Immigration*. N.Y., Macmillan, 1933. pp. 176-185.

Handlin, Oscar. *The Uprooted*. Boston, Little, Brown, 1951. Paperback, Grosset's Universal Library, UL-23. pp. 37-62.

Macbrayne, Lewis E. "Judgment of the Steerage." *Harper's Magazine*, Vol. 117 (September 1908), pp. 489-499.

Steiner, Edward A. *On the Trail of the Immigrant*. N.Y., Revell, 1906.

U.S. Immigration Commission. *Steerage Conditions*. Reports, Vol. 37 (Serial 5877). Abstract in Vol. 2, pp. 295-303.

Whitmarch, Hubert P. "Steerage of Today." *Century*, Vol. 55 (n.s. 33) (February 1898), pp. 528-543.

Chapter 5—First Encounter with the New World

Harrison, Shelby M. "The Anomalous Quarantine Situation in New York Bay." *Survey*, Vol. 27 (January 27, 1912), pp. 1640-1643.

Meyer, Max F. "In Quarantine." *Survey*, Vol. 45 (March 26, 1921), pp. 921-922.

"New York Bay and the Nation's Quarantine." *Survey*, Vol. 28 (April 13, 1912), p. 94.

Salmon, Thomas W. "Federal Quarantine at New York." *Survey*, Vol. 30 (April 26, 1913), pp. 139-140.

Chapters 6-8—Ellis Island Inspection Procedures

Abbott, Ernest H. "America's Welcome to the Immigrant." *Outlook,* Vol. 72 (October 4, 1902), pp. 256-264.

Brandenburg, Broughton. *Imported Americans.* N.Y., Stokes, 1904. pp. 215-227. Same in *Leslie's Monthly Magazine,* Vol. 58 (June 1904), pp. 162-171.

Fairchild, Henry P. *Immigration.* N.Y., Macmillan, 1933. pp. 186-212.

Lowry, Edward A. "Americans in the Raw." *World's Work,* Vol. 4 (October 1902), pp. 2644-2655.

McLaughlin, Allan. "How Immigrants Are Inspected." *Popular Science Monthly,* Vol. 66 (February 1905), pp. 357-361. Same in *Scientific American,* Vol. 59 (March 4, 1905), pp. 24393-24394.

Reed, Alfred C. "Going Through Ellis Island." *Popular Science Monthly,* Vol. 82 (January 1913), pp. 5-18.

Riis, Jacob A. "In the Gateway of Nations." *Century,* Vol. 65 (March 1903), pp. 674-682.

Sweeney, Helen M. "Handling of Immigrants in New York." *Catholic World,* Vol. 63 (July 1896), pp. 497-508.

Watchorn, Robert. "Gateway of the Nation and Enforcement of the Laws." *Outlook,* Vol. 87 (December 28, 1907), pp. 897-912.

Chapter 7—Meeting the Doctors

Abbott, Edith, ed. *Immigration.* Chicago, University of Chicago Press, 1924. pp. 244-251.

McLaughlin, Allan. "Immigration and the Public Health." *Popular Science Monthly,* Vol. 64 (January 1904), pp. 232-238.

Powderly, Terence. "Immigration's Menace to the Public Health." *North American,* Vol. 175 (July 1902), pp. 53-60.

Reed, Alfred C. "Immigration and the Public Health." *Popular Science Monthly,* Vol. 83 (October 1913), pp. 320-338.

Reed, Alfred C. "The Medical Side of Immigration." *Popular Science Monthly,* Vol. 80 (April 1912), pp. 383-392.

Safford, Victor. *Immigration Problems: Personal Experiences of an Official.* N.Y., Dodd Mead, 1925.

Sprague, E. K. "Medical Inspection of Immigrants." *Survey,* Vol. 30 (June 21, 1913), pp. 420-422.

Sprague, E. K. "Mental Examination of Immigrants." *Survey,* Vol. 31 (January 17, 1914), pp. 466-468.

Chapter 8—The Final Barrier
See references under Chapters 6-8 above

Chapter 9—The Detained and Rejected

Howe, Frederic C. "Turned Back in Time of War: Ellis Island Under War Conditions." *Survey*, Vol. 36 (May 6, 1916), pp. 147-156.

Williams, Louis L. "Leak in Quarantine: Stricter Measures Needed on Immigrant Ships." *Survey*, Vol. 33 (December 12, 1914), pp. 291-292.

Chapter 10—Improving the Welcome

Ogg, Frederic A. "New Plan for Immigrant Inspection." *Outlook*, Vol. 83 (May 5, 1906), pp. 33-36.

Sargent, Frank P. "Need for Closer Inspection and Greater Restriction of Immigrants." *Century*, Vol. 67 (January 1904), pp. 470-473.

Information on the many official government investigations may be found in the official records of House and Senate hearings, especially those of 1911, 1916 and 1919.

"Ellis Island Investigation." *Charities and Commons*, Vol. 11 (October 10, 1903), pp. 324-325; Vol. 12 (March 5, 1904), pp. 223-224.

1914—"For a Better Ellis Island." *Outlook*, Vol. 108 (October 21, 1914), pp. 402-403; "Turning Ellis Island Inside Out." *Survey*, Vol. 33 (October 17, 1914), p. 63.

1916—"Bennett-Howe Controversy." *Outlook*, Vol. 113 (August 2, 1916), pp. 763-764.

Howe, Frederic C. "Investigation of Ellis Island Proposed." *Survey*, Vol. 36 (July 29, 1916), pp. 445-446.

1923 (British complaint)—*Literary Digest*, Vol. 78 (September 1, 1923), pp. 17-19; Vol. 78 (September 22, 1923), pp. 23-24.

Chapter 11—Stemming the Flood

Bennett, Marion T. *American Immigration Policies: A History.* Washington, Public Affairs Press, 1963.

Bernard, William S., ed. *American Immigration Policy.* N.Y., Harper, 1950.

"Development of America's Immigration Laws." *Congressional Digest,* Vol. 2 (July-August 1923), pp. 296-298.

Divine, Robert A. *American Immigration Policy, 1924-1952.* New Haven, Yale University Press, 1957.

Handlin, Oscar. *Race and Nationality in American Life.* Boston, Little, Brown, 1957. Paperback, Anchor Books, A 110. pp. 74-110.

Stephenson, George M. *A History of American Immigration, 1820-1924.* Boston, Ginn, 1926. Reprint, N.Y., Russell & Russell, 1964.

Chapter 12—From Ghost Island to National Monument

"Stabilizing the Ruins." *Time,* Vol. 87 (March 4, 1966), p. 78.

Index